Self-Publishing on Amazon 2022

No publisher? No Agent? No Problem!

D0899744

By Dr Andy Williams

ezSEONews.com

Version 1.0

Updated 7th December 2021

Contents

What People Are Saying About Previous Versions of This Book & Andy Williams

"Author was very good in explaining the whole process with tons of details. I had read many eBooks in regards to Kindle Publishing, this is by far the best one." **Fred C**

"I'm reading so many Kindle publishing and formatting books these days to figure out this beast, and this is one of the best. Clear, well organized, well written." **Helen C. Page**

"I liked the most that the author is giving at the very beginning the examples of authors who did exceptionally well with Kindle publishing and then shows his own figures. That for me is great because it is motivating, and I like people who write from their own experience." **Francesca**

"Dr. Andy Williams is someone I have been reading for several years, on a wide variety of Internet-related topics, and I have found him to be knowledgeable and ethical." **Rosana Hart**

"I was actually in the process of publishing a Kindle book when I opened this, and I have to say it's filled out my knowledge in this area better than anything else I have seen or read. It's so complete you may not use it all the very first time you publish, but I think you can go back to it again for more detail as you get more deeply into the process, or publish a second book. Everything is laid out in a step by step way with illustrations." **Inisheer**

"Thank you for this book, Dr. Andy! It is very comprehensive, and I discovered new information that I was previously unaware of. I definitely recommend this book for all Kindle Publishers - it has many great tips and wise advice." **Kerry**

"Andy covers just about every question I had in my mind, as well as quite a few that I hadn't thought of. He does so in an easy to read, relaxed style that demystifies the Kindle publishing process." **Martin Avis**

"What I like about this book is that there are no dirty tricks that could get you in trouble. An easy ABC read for even my 13-year-old who will be writing her own book during half-term." *C. Mulenga*

"Another of Andy's well thought out and executed products. Everything you need to know about publishing and promoting your new book on the Kindle." *Minichester*

"Although I've already published several books on Kindle, there were plenty of great ideas here that I could take away and use. Love the stories at the beginning, followed by practical how-to steps, for each section." *SalisburyOne*

"I've read a lot of info on Kindle publishing and found that this book covers everything from a to z. It's inspired me to have another go as I can see where I went wrong on my first attempt. Time well invested in reading it, IMHO." *Vicky Bellamy*

"Like many, I have read several books on Kindle publishing. Some go into mind-numbing detail, and others are lightweight. Andy has got the balance absolutely right for newbie (Kindle) authors. An excellent read with great content and several web links to useful resources." *Keith Finney*

Disclaimer and Terms of Use Agreement

A Note About UK v US English

There are some differences between UK and US English. While I try to be consistent, some errors may slip into my writing because I spend a lot of time corresponding with people in both the UK and the US. The line can blur.

Examples of this include the spelling of words like optimise (UK) v optimize (US).

The difference I get the most complaints about is with collective nouns. Collective nouns refer to a group of individuals, e.g., Google. In the US, collective nouns are singular, so **Google IS** a company. However, in the UK, collective nouns are usually plural, so **Google ARE** a company. This is not to be confused with Google, "the search engine," which is obviously singular in both.

There are other differences too. I hope that if I have been inconsistent anywhere in this book, it does not detract from the value you get from it.

Found Typos in This Book?

Errors can get through proof-readers, so if you do find any typos or grammatical errors in this book, I'd be very grateful if you could let me know using this email address:

typos@ezseonews.com

URLs in This Book

Ideally, I would love it if everyone could click a URL to be taken to a web page referenced in this book. However, I realize that paperback books don't offer such a luxury.

So, whenever I link to a web page with a long URL, I'll use a shortened version of the URL to make it easier to type in. All the redirected URLs will begin with https://ezseonews.com/, followed by a short identifier. Ezseonews.com is my domain, which means I can easily manage these redirect URLs if they change in the future.

There are several different reasons why the sale of eBooks, eReaders, and tablets is booming. For a start, eBooks are greener, cheaper, and more convenient. Electronic publishing reduces the consumption of natural resources and the level of pollution too because it does not incur the costs that traditional printing does. As a result, the price of eBooks is considerably lower than that of traditional paper books.

Instead of piling up physical books at home, readers build up a virtual library that is light, transportable, and easily manageable. An eBook comes with additional features, such as text search, highlights, bookmarks, and notes. What's more, an eBook is instantly available and is just a click away, thanks to online shopping.

Browsing the online bookstores and finding the right book has proven to be a much more efficient way to shop for an average reader. And the ever-growing number of available digital books provides a broad range of titles. Books in certain niches and specialty books are so much easier to find on the internet than in the high street, and the buyer can purchase worldwide.

The flourishing market for eBooks and eReaders has opened a whole new world for authors. Most of all, writers have welcomed the possibility of self-publishing their work in the form of electronic books. Self-publishing represents a challenging alternative to traditional publishing in the sense that it gives the writer more freedom, flexibility, and visibility. Higher revenues, sole copyrights, freedom of choice (regarding format and design), quick access to the marketplace, and direct contact with the readers, are just some of the appealing aspects of self-publishing as opposed to traditional publishing. So, how does the growing trend of eBooks and eReaders help all those who would like to venture into digital self-publishing?

First, authors have the option to bridge the gap between themselves and the readers by publishing their books online without the use of publishers as intermediaries. Instead, authors can reach the global marketplace quickly and effectively by using one of the publishing platforms, such as Amazon's Kindle, Barnes and Noble's Nook Press, Apple's iBookstore, or Google Book. All these platforms are free to use. Authors just sign up, upload their eBook, and receive royalties from the platform, varying between 40% and 80%. Some of these platforms will even auto-convert uploaded eBooks into their own format and paperback.

Following this self-publishing route, authors no longer need to find a publisher to accept their book. Now, they simply upload their work to the different platforms, and within hours, their book is available for sale. If they are very successful, they still have the option to publish a hardback or a paperback edition with a publishing company (this is the route taken by E. L. James with her 50 Shades trilogy). Furthermore, editors, proofreaders, and graphic designers, necessary for a traditional book, are not essential when self-publishing. Depending on the budget and the topic, authors can search the internet for available services or do most of the formatting and design work themselves. In contrast to traditional publishing, self-published authors retain their copyrights and thereby considerably increase their own revenues once their eBooks are sold.

A huge success story in the self-publishing world is Smashwords. Founded in 2008, Smashwords is the "world's largest distributor of indie eBooks," and .".make it fast and free for anyone, anywhere in the world, to publish and distribute eBooks to major retailers and thousands of libraries."

At Smashwords, authors can get 80% of the net revenues from the sale of their books, and they still retain all the rights. Contrary to the earlier prejudices against self-publishers, the latest developments with platforms such as Smashwords prove that self-published books are gaining more and more visibility. Library Direct is the project launched by Smashwords for big libraries and databases to gain access to books published on Smashwords.

Authors who turn to self-publishing will need to carefully structure their marketing plan. Since there's no big publishing company in charge of publicity, the writers themselves must use all the available channels of communication to promote the sale of their books. This can include social media like Facebook and Twitter (though in truth, this often becomes more important as you "grow" as an author). Many "indie" writers set up a website or blog which can be used to promote their books and communicate with their audience.

The boom in e-publishing not only represents a great advantage for those in need of a mobile and easily accessible library but also a massive opportunity for those who want to publish their own work.

While digital eBooks will continue to offer self-published authors a great opportunity, I recommend you publish in **both digital and paperback** versions because there isn't a lot of extra work to do this. This book has you covered. In it, I will show you how to publish both digital and paperback versions, so your books are available in both formats on the biggest online bookstore in the world - Amazon.

Before we look at the mechanics of self-publishing, I want to talk a little about some success stories.

Successful Self-Published Authors

J. A. Konrath

You can find his website here:

https://jakonrath.com/

.. and his blog here:

https://jakonrath.blogspot.com/

J. A. Konrath's blog is a mine of information. For many years, he updated what he calls *"Konrath's resolutions for writers,"* which serves as a testimony of how much the book industry has changed since 2006, notably with the advent of e-books. Go to his site and search for it. It's well worth a read and does the author great credit to not have erased a single entry on the list, and to include sentences such as this: *"I've lived long enough to see my advice become obsolete, and that gives me hope for the future."* Not surprisingly, Konrath has embraced the new possibilities that e-books offer, such as the opportunity to self-publish on Amazon and not grieving the loss of an old-world, but welcoming change.

The man behind the blog is a writer with a good heart who believes in a community of writers lending each other a hand. He teaches writing at Dupage College, Illinois, and has written fiction under the pen names Jack Kilborn, Joe Kimball, and of course, his own name J. A. Konrath. He likes to write horror (usually under the pen name Jack Kilborn), with titles like *Afraid* and *Trapped*. The series of novels popularly known as the *"Jack Daniels"* series (including *Whiskey Sour* or *Rusty Nail)* are some of his top sellers. He describes his own work as *"A cross between the scares of Thomas Harris and the laughs of Dave Barry."*

After reading about him and the way he struggled through the endless rejections of his first nine novels, many writers would have felt depressed and defeated. However, J.A. Konrath's message to aspiring writers is that it is possible to make a living as a genre fiction writer. His optimism is backed by useful tips on how to self-publish in a more effective way.

Spend some time on his blog and read his tips and motivational pieces. After reading his blog, you should be left with one overwhelming message. If you are not enjoying success, you cannot blame anyone but yourself. Write a good book, turn it into an e-book, and make it available online. Oh, and make sure you do it NOW!

John Locke

John Locke's story is a little old now, but one that got me interested in self-publishing.

Some stories are worth reading because they take you, the reader, into a sequence of action and suspense scenes where you don't know what is going to happen next. It might be late at night, and you might have to get up early for work the next day, but your mind craves another page, or perhaps just another paragraph – but you need to know what happens next. This quality is what John Locke describes as "punch." He wants his stories to have "punch," and most of his readers agree that they do.

John Locke is the best-selling author of lots of novels and a book of non-fiction about how to sell e-books. His best-known works are the *Donovan Creed* novels. Starting with *Lethal People,* Mr. Locke introduces Donovan Creed, an ex-CIA agent who works for an obscure agency. Despite seeming like a classic "tough guy" and being a ruthless murderer, when necessary, Donovan has a heart and a way with women. He has, of course, written other books, like *Emmet & Gentry,* or *Bad Doctor* - and created some other well-crafted characters like *Emmet Love* or *Dani Ripper*. This combination of "punch" and appealing characters is Mr. Locke's formula for producing one page-turner after another. In 2011 alone, he wrote nine books.

John Locke's story is an interesting one.

He began writing fiction to relax after having open-heart surgery. He enjoyed it so much that he decided to try self-publishing his work in print. This was at a great personal cost and with little success. Then, in March 2010, he decided to e-publish the same three novels and sell each book for only 99 cents on Amazon. By 2011, his sales had reached huge figures, and one of his novels, *Saving Rachel*, had even reached number 1 on Amazon. His promotional strategy was simple. An attractive cover and product description. A well-edited final product. Effective self-promotion on social networks like Facebook and Twitter.

You can read John Locke's blog here:

https://johnlockeauthor.wordpress.com/

You'll notice that John doesn't post very often on his blog. His strategy is to write a blog post that will resonate with his target audience and then draw them to the blog post via social channels like Twitter. If you are part of his target audience, the chances are that his blog posts will resonate with you. They'll bring out emotions as you read them, and this is what he wants. He wants that connection with his readers. It's much easier to sell to someone when you have that connection. John's strategy is all about building those relationships, and it doesn't matter what business you are in. It's a smart way to go if you can pull it off.

Amanda Hocking

Here is Amanda's website:

http://hockingbooks.com/

Her life story is interesting. It tells of a penniless young lady living in Austin, Minnesota, and how she spent late nights writing book after book in an effort to be published by the end of 2009. Like many aspiring authors, her efforts resulted in a lot of rejection letters from various publishing houses. In 2010, Amanda found out about Elisa Lorello and her novel entitled 'Faking It.' That book had made it into the top 100 on Kindle, and Elisa did it without a publisher. Things quickly started falling into place as Amanda discovered other successful self-published authors (including J.A. Konrath).

Although still not totally convinced about self-publishing, Amanda decided to give it a go. There was a Jim Henson exhibit coming to Chicago later in the year, and she wanted to go. She decided to try self-publishing to see if she could raise enough money to cover the costs of attending the Muppet exhibition. All she needed was a couple of hundred bucks.

The rest is history!

Amanda made the "couple hundred bucks" to go to the exhibit. In fact, she made a lot more.

In June 2010, she made $3180.

In July 2010, she made $6527.

In August 2010, she was on track to make $9000 - $10,000.

Compare this to her previous year's income. In 2009, working her day job, Amanda grossed $18,000.

If you check Amanda's Wikipedia entry, you'll get a few more stats on her. Here is an amazing stat that will surely inspire you:

By March 2011, she had sold over a million copies of her nine books and earned two million dollars from the sales. In early 2011, she was averaging 9,000 book sales a day!

Amanda's massive success was down to her decision to take the self-publishing route!

Amanda Hocking has become a prophet of change in the book world, despite her own reluctance to accept such an honor. Despite the popularity her work has earned her, it is safe to say she will not be remembered so much for it, as for the implications her success has had for the very foundations of the publishing industry. Her example is already being followed by thousands of other writers, tired of facing constant setbacks and rejection from publishing houses.

In March 2011, Miss Hocking signed a contract with St. Martin's Press for 4 of her books. It was a deal worth 2 million US dollars. Would she ever have signed a contract like this if she had not already become hugely successful as a self-published author?

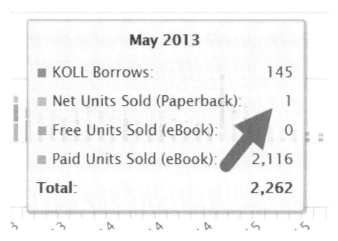

By August 2013, paperback sales had really taken off:

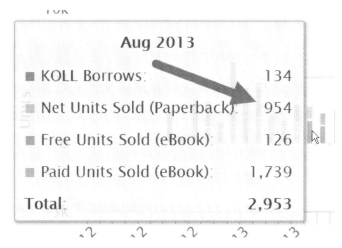

Today, most of my sales are paperbacks rather than Kindle, though I am sure that is because I write non-fiction, tutorial-style books that people want open in front of them while working on their computer.

Here is the actual income I received during those first few months as a self-published author:

August 2012 - $6.27

September 2012 - $278.09

October 2012 - $1492.66

November 2012 - $1958.73

December 2012 - $2989.18

That's from zero to nearly $3000 a month in 5 months working part-time. That income was mainly from 3 books, but that was only the start.

Today I have over 20 books in both Kindle and paperback versions. Some of these books have been updated and re-released each year. I am sure you will understand why I don't share later data, but if it wasn't worth it, I wouldn't still be doing it.

But Success Isn't Guaranteed

This sounds like a strange thing to be telling you before you even start self-publishing, but it's true. I make good money from my self-published books, but it was a lot of work, experimentation, sweat, and tears. One thing I have learned is that having a great book is not enough. I have a few books that I think are great, but they don't sell at all. I have other books that I think are great that do. So, what is the difference?

The most important thing that will make your book sell, or not, is whether there is a pre-existing audience for it. You can write the best, most authoritative and entertaining book on the mating habits of earthworms, but if nobody is interested, it won't sell.

No one wants to invest weeks of work into a book that flops. To be brutally honest, there is no sure-fire way of knowing whether a book will sell or not, but there are some very good indicators we can look at, and this is where we'll start our journey by using Amazon as a research tool.

Using Amazon for **Research**

Amazon provides us with a lot of useful information about our intended genre or niche. We can use it to learn about the competition we face and whether or not there is an audience for our intended work. Using Amazon, we can find out if a particular book is selling and roughly estimate how many sales it makes each day. This can be useful information for authors because we can see whether a book we want to write is likely to have an audience. Think about it. If you knew that books in your chosen niche weren't selling, would you still write the book?

Similarly, if you were looking for a topic to write about, then seeing books selling very well in a particular niche would be interesting. We'll look at the kind of information we can get on 'any book' on Amazon shortly. First, I want to show you a cool way to brainstorm book ideas.

Amazon's Auto-Complete Search Box

Amazon's search box tries to complete what you type. If I go over there and start to type in the word "zombies," look what happens:

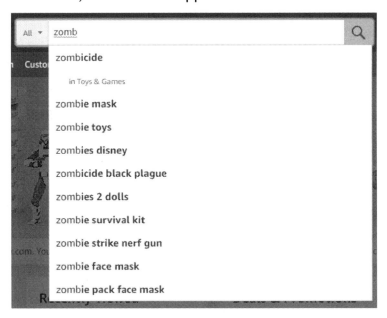

Amazon lists the phrases that it thinks I might be interested in.

Where does it get these phrases from?

Well, Amazon isn't telling, but I'd bet it was based on search queries that previous visitors had typed in, with the most typed search phrases at the top!

This can be a great tool for niche research, especially if we narrow our search to the books department. After all, we are only really interested in the books that Amazon customers are searching for. You can see these suggestions are different from those we received when searching all departments earlier.

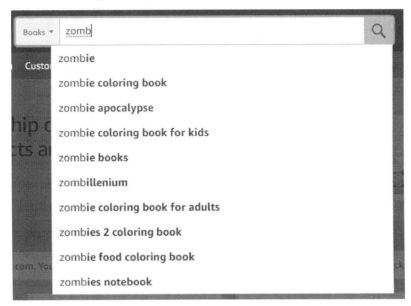

And you'll get slightly different suggestions if you search in the Kindle section of Amazon:

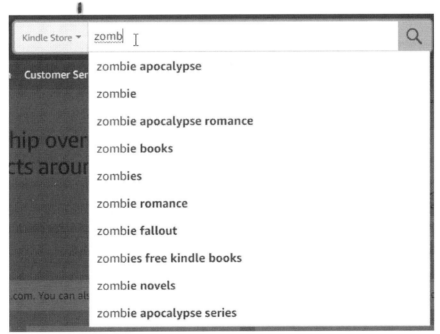

I can see right there that my idea for a zombie apocalypse book would probably have an audience!

Looking at the order of the phrases, they are clearly not alphabetical. It makes sense that these would be in the order of search volume. I mean, Amazon wants to provide you with suggestions, so why not put the most popular suggestions at the top of the list. It makes sense, doesn't it? Therefore, we can see which of the phrases are more popular. That's a great start for our niche/genre research.

One thing to bear in mind is that the autocomplete suggestions you are seeing are the same auto-complete suggestions other visitors will see.

Why is that useful to remember?

Well, when you are looking for "search keywords" for your book (see later), then choosing phrases that appear in these lists is a smart way to go. Think about it for a minute. A lot of people will end up clicking on one of the auto-complete suggestions, meaning they end up searching for that term. If your book is ranking for that search term, then you've just delivered eyeballs to your book cover. By using phrases from this auto-complete feature, you don't have to second guess what people are searching for. You just need to take Amazon's suggestions and make sure you rank for those phrases.

You can extract a huge amount of information from an auto-complete search tool by structuring your search. Look what happens when I type the letter "a" after the word "zombie":

Amazon tries to complete the phrase even though I've only typed an "a." What we end up with is a lot of phrases that people are searching for, starting with "zombie a." What if you repeated this search with "zombie b" or "zombie c"?

Go on, try it!

You can go through the entire alphabet to find some really great book ideas.

Here's one that's interesting:

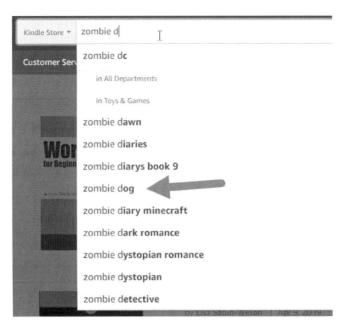

Zombies don't always have to be human (or should I say ex-human). There seems to be a market for zombie dog stories. Or perhaps there is a well-known zombie dog series that people are searching for?

Bob the Zombie Dog
by Benjamin James | Jan 26, 2021
Kindle Edition
Ages: 0 - 6 years

Hounded Book 3: There's more blood...more guts...more glory! (Hou world, terrifying 3-part serial horror thriller!)
by Ellie Douglas | Jan 25, 2021
Kindle Edition

Well, I didn't expect that!

Do you see how valuable this type of research is?

There are loads of small niches within larger genres, and if you find one with a rabid audience (pun intended), so much the better.

Besides getting great ideas for books, these auto-complete search phrases are excellent keywords to keep for later. When you submit your book, you'll need to enter suggested "search keywords." Therefore, keep a list of relevant search terms for later reference.

We can also determine whether there is an existing audience for our books by spying on our would-be competitors.

Let's use Amazon for that.

Competitor Research

In the search box at the top, select **Kindle Store** and enter the phrase you want to research. Amazon will show you your competition as a set of search results. You can quickly check the price of competing books and see if these books are getting many reviews. However, the real research begins when we click through to one of the book's product pages.

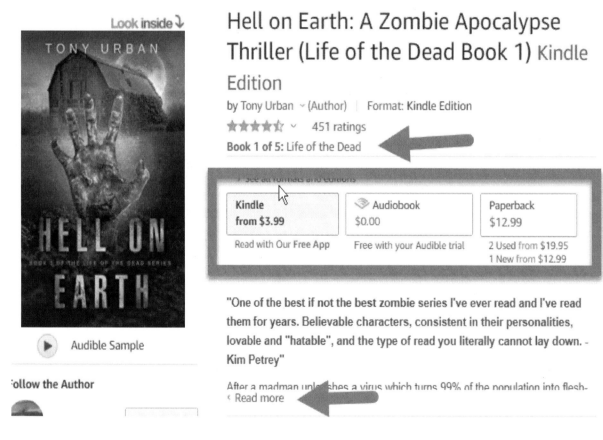

I can quickly see that this book is part of a series. It's book one of five. I can also see that this book is available as a Kindle, Audiobook, and paperback.

The book description is worth reading, as it will give you an idea of what is selling in this niche (assuming this book does sell, and we'll discover that in a moment). You might also pick up on some words or phrases being used that you can add to your list of relevant keywords.

Under the description, you may see the other books in the series:

This is useful because you can see the prices of the books in the series, as well as customer review rating. If I was going to write a zombie book, I might be tempted to buy the first one in the series to see why the books are getting such great reviews. I might even be hooked into the world and buy all five! It's all valuable research.

Further down the page, you can see a really useful section called "Customers who viewed this item also viewed."

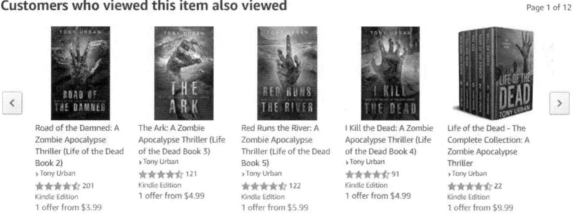

This is great information to have because it gives you more examples of what people are looking for in this genre.

OK, now for the most important bit. We know this book has great reviews, but when was it released, and is it still selling? How many pages does the book contain? Is it long or short?

Scroll down to the **Product Details** section of the page:

Product details

ASIN : B01M74LQTO

Publisher : Packanack Publishing (November 8, 2016)

Publication date : November 8, 2016 ←

Language : English

File size : 2038 KB

Simultaneous device usage : Unlimited

Text-to-Speech : Enabled

Screen Reader : Supported

Enhanced typesetting : Enabled

X-Ray : Enabled

Word Wise : Enabled

Print length : 257 pages ←

Best Sellers Rank: #6,070 in Kindle Store (See Top 100 in Kindle Store) ←
   #2 in Teen & Young Adult Zombie Fiction
   #23 in Science Fiction (Kindle Store)
   #36 in U.S. Horror Fiction

Customer Reviews: ★★★★☆ ˅   451 ratings

At the top, we can see this book as published in 2016. That is over four years ago, so it has been around for a while. We can also see that the book is estimated as being 257 pages in length. This is an estimate because we are dealing with a Kindle book where there are no actual pages. The paperback version should show a more accurate value, and that says 247 pages.

This is useful information because we can then tell whether the books that are selling are long or short. For example, if I wanted to write a comprehensive book on baking but saw that all of the baking books that sold well were actually quite short, then that would suggest I might be better off splitting my book into smaller, niche baking guides.

The page length coupled with the cost of the book can also help guide us when we come to price our own publication.

At the bottom of the **Product Details** is the **Best Sellers Rank**. This one ranks 6,070 in the paid Kindle store. That means there are only 6,069 books on Kindle that sell more than this one. Is that good? Well, we'll see in a moment. For now, just remember that the lower the Amazon Best Sellers Rank number is, the more that book sells.

When you are researching competing books, you might see that the Amazon Best Sellers Rank looks a little different.

Best Sellers Rank: #1 Free in Kindle Store (See Top 100 in Kindle Store)
  1 in Whispersync for Voice (Kindle St...
  1 in Contemporary Romance (Kindle Store)
  1 in Military Romance (Kindle Store)
Customer reviews: ★★★★☆ ∨   1,099 ratings

This book is ranked #1 Free in Kindle Store.

As we'll see later, you can give your book away for free, and this one is clearly doing that at the moment. Amazon ranks free books in a separate chart. This one ranks #1 in that chart, so only no other free book is being downloaded more often than this one. But despite all the downloads, the author is not making any money from this promotion. We'll see later why this type of promotion can be great in other ways.

It is easier to rank in the free charts than the paid section, so you can largely ignore any seller ranks in the free Kindle store. They do not give you an idea of potential sales.

At the very bottom of the product detail section, you'll see the categories where the current book ranks.

Best Sellers Rank: #6,870 in Kindle Store (See Top 100 in Kindle Store)
  #2 in Teen & Young Adult Zombie Fiction
  #23 in Science Fiction (Kindle Store)
  #36 in U.S. Horror Fiction
Customer Reviews: ★★★★☆ ∨   451 ratings

These categories can give you an idea of categories for your own book, but there is a problem. When you come to submit your book, the categories available are not the same ones you see in these product detail listings. We'll come back to that later.

The customer reviews are also really useful for research. Reviews offer feedback from people that read the book. Spend time going through the reviews of competing books and making notes on what people liked, what they disliked, and what they wished the book had included. When you write your book, you can make sure you don't make the same mistakes as these other authors. At the same time, you can include any good ideas.

Have a look to see what other information is available on each of your competitor's product pages. The information changes frequently, but I have covered the main areas that I look at when researching a book. Now, let's find out what the Amazon Best Sellers Rank really means in terms of sales.

Making Sense of the Sales Rank

The first thing to know is that the Best Sellers Rank (BSR) is calculated independently at each of the Amazon stores. The #1 bestseller on Amazon.co.uk will sell a lot less than the #1 bestseller on Amazon.com, even though they have the same BSR.

The other thing to remember is that Kindle, paperback, and audiobook versions of the book will each have their own bestseller rank, telling you how popular that format is for the book.

Remember, BSR is the rank order of how books sell. A BSR of 1 means it's the top-selling book on Amazon. A BSR of 10,000 means it's the 10,000th best-selling book on Amazon.

The figures I am going to give here refer to Amazon.com only. If you want to estimate book sales from Best Seller Rank, go to Amazon.com to check out the ranks there.

Amazon doesn't tell us how BSR translates into sales volume, and this isn't a fixed value anyway. If Amazon has a slower day, the #1 bestseller rank will sell fewer books than the #1 bestseller rank on a great sales day.

However, a number of people (myself included) have recorded their own sales volume and corresponding sales rank average. There are also a few online tools that can give estimates. The problem for me is that some of these online tools don't correlate very well with what I have seen from my own book sales.

Here are conservative estimates based on my own book sales.

The first number is the Amazon Best Sellers Rank, and the number in brackets is the number of books sold in a 24-hour period.

50,000 (0-1)

30,000 (2-3)

20,000 (4-5)

10,000 (8-10)

5,000 (20-25)

4,000 (30-34)

So, if you have a sales rank of 10,000, chances are you are selling around 8 – 10 books a day. With a sales rank of around 5,000, that number jumps to 20-25 sales per day. These numbers are only estimates based on my own sales, and they are far more conservative than you will get with online BSR calculators you can find online.

I can only guess at sales volume for sellers ranks better than 4,000. After reading other people's experiences, I'd expect something like this:

1,000 (100)

500 (200)

1 (3000+)

Again, I need to repeat that these figures are based on educated guesswork and listening to other authors.

Using the information in this section, you can estimate how many sales a particular book makes. If your competitor is making good sales, then you know there is a market for books on that topic.

As an example, that zombie book has a BSR of 6,070. That translates into around 18-20 sales a day. Multiply that by the royalty rate the book gets (70% of $3.99), and you can estimate how much money the author is making. In this case, probably around $50 a day.

Potential Profits from Kindle Book Sales

When you sell a book on Amazon Kindle, Amazon pays you a royalty.

The value of the royalty is a percentage of the sale after any deductions for download bandwidth. The fee Amazon charges for each download of your book depends on the size of your book in megabytes (MB). You won't get charged this fee on smaller books (or free books), but as the book size increases, Amazon starts to deduct a delivery fee out of the purchase price.

Before we look at delivery costs, it's important to understand the royalty structure. This can also change, so for the most up-to-date information, do check with Amazon.

There are two Royalty "options" - 70% or 35%.

If your Kindle book is priced between $2.99 and $9.99, then you are eligible for 70% royalties, except in certain circumstances. For example, sales in certain countries will only result in 35% royalties. However, to complicate things, 70% royalties may be possible in some countries, but only if your book is enrolled in KDP. We'll discuss KDP later in the promotion section.

If your book is outside that price range (higher or lower), then you get 35% royalties on all sales. There are no download fees on books where the royalty is 35%.

On sales that qualify for the 70% royalty, there may be a download charge. The charge is similar in all countries and in the US. It is equal to $0.15 per MB at the time of writing. Therefore, if your book is 3MB in size (which it might be if you have a lot of images or photos), then the delivery charge on each sale that is eligible for 70% royalties will be 3 x $0.15 = $0.45.

For more details on book pricing and royalties, see these pages on Amazon:

1. Pricing Page: https://ezseonews.com/kdp-dpp
2. Sales & Royalties FAQ: https://ezseonews.com/kdp-ero

For paperbacks, the royalty rate is 60%, and rather than download fees to contend with, you have printing costs, which are taken out of your 60%!

Here is an example from one of my own paperbacks:

As you can see, the normal commission rate is 60%, after printing costs. Expanded distribution allows your books to be distributed to bookstores, online retailers, libraries, and academic institutions. That channel only offers a 40% commission.

So, let's do the calculation on this $8.99 paperback. Amazon works out the 60% commission ($5.39) and subtracts printing costs to leave $2.72 per paperback sale of this book. In this case, that is around 30% of the sale price.

You may be disappointed with that, but you do not have to pay for your book to be published or commissions to an agent or publishing house. It is 100% free. You will not get a bill from Amazon, just monthly commission deposits into your bank account. You are also on the biggest bookstore in the world, visible by countries across the globe.

We'll come back to pricing later. For now, your next step is to write your book. In the following section, we'll look at how you should format your book.

Writing & Formatting Your Book

A popular tool for writers is Scrivener. It's a dedicated writing tool for Windows and Mac users. I own a copy of Scrivener myself but don't use it. My tool of choice for self-publishing is Microsoft Word. However, you can use pretty much any software tool for writing your book, including any of the free office suites like Open Office, Libre Office, Google Docs, etc.

If you don't have a good word processor yet, I would recommend you check out SoftMaker's Free Office. It is an excellent suite of tools that are fully compatible with Microsoft Office and free! Search Google for it.

I'll be sticking with Microsoft Word in this book, and if you own Microsoft Word, I highly recommend you use it too.

If you are an experienced word processor user, a lot of the formatting we do in this book will seem obvious. Don't just skip these sections, though, because there are some basic formatting styles we need to adhere to for electronic books.

Creating a Style for your Books

Before I started publishing books on Amazon, I set up a Word "Style" that could accommodate how I wanted to do things. You can do a very similar process in any Word processor.

I'll show you how to set this up in Microsoft Word.

If you are new to Word and don't have a preferred setup in terms of fonts, paragraphs, alignment, margins, etc., then I suggest you start off by selecting one of the presets built into Word and modify that.

You can do this by clicking on the **Design** tab.

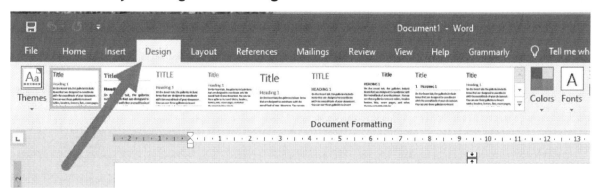

There are several ready-made document formatting styles that you can select. There are also a few different **Themes** that you can choose from.

Let me show you how to set this up.

From the **Themes** menu, select **Office.**

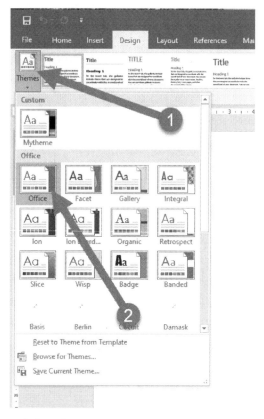

Each theme in that list will load its own unique set of document formatting styles, which you can view by mousing over them in the **Document Formatting** window:

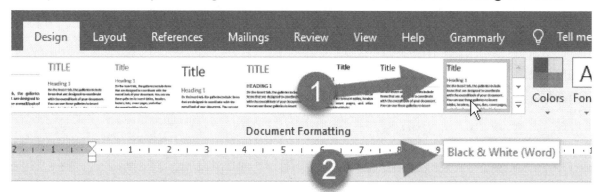

As your mouse moves from one to the next, the text in your Word document will update to show you that style. You will also get a tooltip to tell you the name of the style you are viewing.

Select **Black & White (Word).**

This gives us a starting point to create our own style.

Which Font?

When writing your book, stick to a plain and simple font and never mix two or more fonts within the same document. Amazon Kindle will over-write your font(s) anyway, but that may not be the case with other eBook publishing platforms, and it certainly isn't the case when you publish your book as a paperback. Get into the habit of using a single font throughout.

Font size is not critical for Kindle versions because Kindle owners can change the font size on their device. However, if you are going to be creating a paperback from your Word document, it is important. Therefore, I suggest you set up Word to use the correct font sizes from the beginning.

If you want to read some thoughts on fonts, look at this article – Picking Fonts for your Self-Published Book:

https://ezseonews.com/kdp-pickfonts

Please note that you can't just use any font. You need to make sure you have the right to use the font commercially. I am not a lawyer, so please don't ask my advice on this. You need to read the copyright information of the fonts you have access to. Having said that, any fonts that came pre-installed with Word are probably safe to use.

There are a couple of places you can find free fonts for commercial use:

1. https://www.exljbris.com/
2. https://www.fontsquirrel.com/

Quick Style Buttons

On the **Home** tab in Word, the ribbon bar has "buttons" for quickly selecting styles for the text in your book.

If you select any text in your Word document, the styles panel will highlight the currently used style for the selected text. Click on one of these style buttons to change a style, and the text will be formatted accordingly. e.g., if you click on Heading 3, the selected text will be styled the way your theme has set up the formatting for Heading 3.

Try it. Select some text in your document.

Click the **Heading 1** button, and the selected text will become a large heading. Click on **Normal**, and your selected text will be formatted as "normal" text.

The main paragraphs in your book should always be formatted to the "Normal" style:

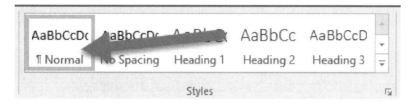

You can test this by clicking on a paragraph of your book, and the Normal format should become highlighted:

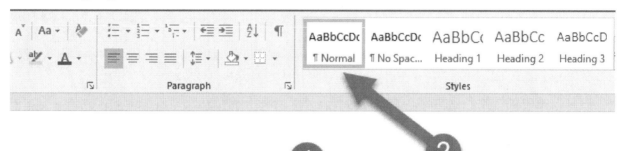

You can see where I have clicked into the paragraph, and the **Normal** format is highlighted.

The main formatting styles I use in my books are as follows:

• **Normal** – For the main text of the book.

• **No Spacing** –for problems with some justified text that tries to stretch a few words across an entire line. I set this style to left-aligned to prevent these issues.

• **Heading 1** – For chapter headings.

• **Heading 2** – For the main sub-headers in the chapter.

• **Heading 3** – For sub-sections of the main chapter sections.

• **Title** – For the title on the cover page.

• **Subtitle** – For the subtitle/tagline on the cover page.

• **Quote** – For quoting people, websites, or other sources.

You need to make sure that all these formats are set up to use your chosen font.

Quickly Changing the Default Font for your Style

You can quickly change the font used in a style by clicking the **Fonts** button over on the **Design** tab:

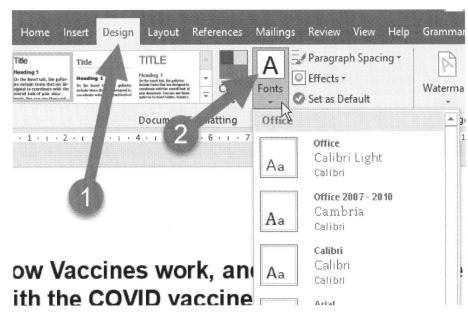

Select the font you want to use, and all styles will be updated to use that font.

For now, select the Office font, Calibri Light, at the top.

OK, all styles now use this font. However, this does not change the color or size of the text. We need to do that manually.

To do that, go back to the Home tab and right-click on the **Normal** style button, and select the **Modify** option:

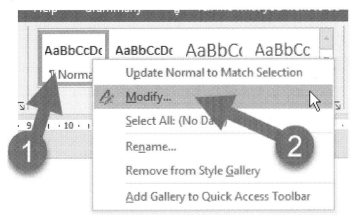

This opens a dialogue box that allows you to change the font style:

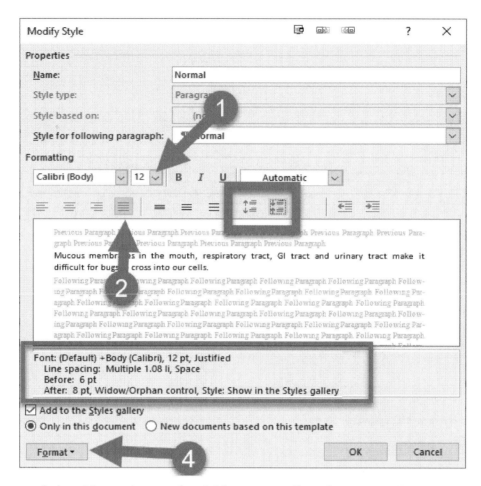

I'd recommend that **Normal** text should be no smaller than size 12.

Notice that you can also change the alignment of the text, and if you want your paragraphs justified, select the justify button. On the same toolbar, there are two buttons you can click to adjust the spacing between paragraphs. One increases the gap between paragraphs, and the other decreases it. This is the correct way to ensure the spacing between paragraphs is correct. Never type hard line-breaks to leave a space.

At the bottom, you can see the format specifications as you make the changes. You can see mine now has the 12pt font, justified with line spacing set to 1.08. There is also a 6pt space before each paragraph and an 8pt space after each paragraph.

These are good settings for the Normal style.

This is almost how I want my paragraphs displayed, with one small change. I want my line spacing a little more than 1.08. I want to set this as 1.15. To do this, click the Format button at the bottom left and select **Paragraph** from the menu. This opens up a new screen that allows us to refine the formatting.

Select **Multiple** from the line spacing drop-down box and set that to 1.15.

Click OK to close this dialogue box, and OK to close the **Modify Style** screen.

We now need to set the sizes of the headers (Heading 1, Heading 2, and Heading 3 are usually the only ones I use in my books). To do this, just right-click the style button and select Modify for each header in turn.

Here are my settings for Heading 3:

Font: (Default) +Headings (Calibri Light), 14 pt, Bold, Font color: Text 1, Space
   Before: 8 pt
   After: 6 pt, Keep with next, Keep lines together, Level 3, Style: Linked, Hide until used,
Show in the Styles gallery, Priority: 10

I've set the size to 14 and made the heading bold and color black. I've also clicked the button to increase the space before and after the headline. I have 8 points before, 6 points afterward.

I always add two points to my "normal" text size to use as the Heading 3. I'll then add two more for heading 2 and two more for heading 1. This is just personal preference, but here is a quick reference for those sizes:

Normal text – 12

Heading 1 - 18

Heading 2 - 16

Heading 3 - 14

Here are my H2 settings:

Font: 16 pt, Bold, Font color: Text 1, Space
   Before: 8 pt
   After: 6 pt, Keep with next, Keep lines together, Level 2, Style: Linked, Hide until used,
Show in the Styles gallery, Priority: 10

Here are my H1 settings:

Font: (Default) +Headings (Calibri Light), 18 pt, Bold, Font color: Text 1, Space
   Before: 18 pt
   After: 6 pt, Keep with next, Keep lines together, Level 1, Style: Linked, Show in the Styles
gallery, Priority: 10

Obviously, you need to decide on these for yourself and what works best with the type of book you are writing, but the headings are hierarchical, so the Heading 1 should be bigger than Heading 2, which is bigger than Heading 3. Heading 3 should be bigger than the main text to make sure the headers stand out.

OK, you can now save your style.

On the Design tab, in the bottom right corner of the **Document Formatting** options, there is a button:

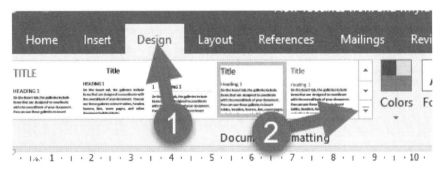

Click it.

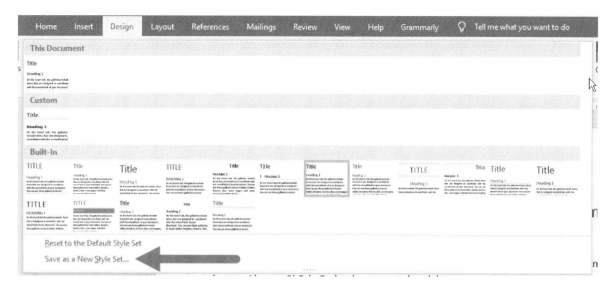

On the drop-down menu that appears, click on the **Save as a New Style Set...** option.

Give your style a name, e.g., Kindle Books, and save it.

You can now see that style added to the Custom section of the menu:

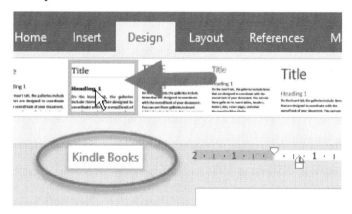

The style will now be available whenever you start a new book. Just select it, and your formatting and style options will be loaded for your new book.

If you want to format a pre-existing document, then after you load your book into Word, just go and select your style from the drop-down menu, then save your book again.

The Essential Sections of your Book

When you create a book, there are a few special pages that you need to think about in the manuscript, either before or after the main book content. What you include may depend on whether your book is fiction or non-fiction. Let's look at these special pages. You can refer to the corresponding sections of this book if you want an example.

Before the Main Book Content

1. Cover Page – This page shows the title, subtitle, author, and version or release date. At the end of the cover page content, insert a page break.

2. Disclaimer and Terms of Use – a legal disclaimer that essentially disclaims liability for the information in the book and confirms copyright. You can find examples if you search Google.

3. Extra Information - This can be anything you want your readers to be aware of. It might be a "How to use this book" paragraph for non-fiction books or a list of "testimonials" you've received for the book. One bit of information I like to include is an email address with a request for readers to report typos and errors. You'll also see that this book explains why I have shortened URLs in some cases.

After the Main Book Content

1. Useful Resources – If you have resources you want to tell your readers about, include them in a resource section. This can include other books you've written, courses, websites, etc.

2. Ask for a review – Reviews are everything on Amazon. You have to be careful in how you ask, but there is nothing wrong with saying something like, "If you enjoyed this book, please consider leaving an honest review on Amazon."

3. An Index – If you are writing non-fiction books and plan to publish as a paperback, you might want to consider an index page. Word does have features to help you manage these, though making a useful index is a time-consuming activity. I haven't included one in this book but may consider adding one in time.

Important Formatting Rules

With the style set up and ready for us, let's look at how we use these formatting options to create a single manuscript that can be used to generate both Kindle and Paperback versions of the book.

Headings

The types of headings you will include in your book vary, depending on the type of book you are writing. If you are a fiction writer, then headings may be limited to Chapter headings and possibly a few other sections in the book, like "About the Author" or "More books by the author."

If you are a non-fiction writer, headings are usually nested. Typically, each chapter will start with a large header (heading 1) and may then be broken down into sub-sections, each with its own heading (heading 2).

In Word Processors, headers are usually defined by a number. Header 1 is the largest, then header 2, header 3, header 4, and so on.

All main section headings in your book (like the start of each chapter) should be the Header 1 level (the largest).

If you divide your main sections into smaller sections, then these should be Level 2. Any sub-headings within the sub-headings should be level 3. I probably wouldn't go deeper than three nested levels.

Adding headings in your book is easy. Simply select the text you want to change to a heading, and click on the heading style you want from the **Styles** selector:

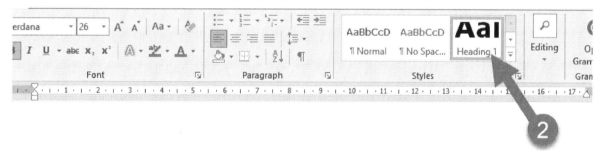

In other word processors, this may look a little different. In Libre Office, for example, it looks like this:

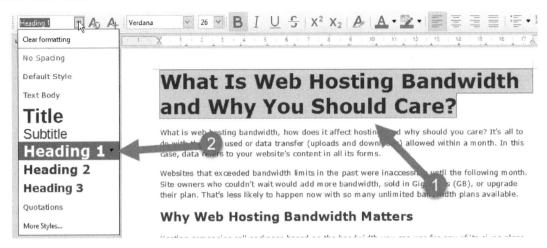

The process of creating a heading is the same in Libre Office. You first select the text and then set the formatting by choosing it from this drop-down style box.

Paragraphs, Carriage Returns, and Page Breaks

When it comes to paragraphs and carriage returns, there is a very important rule. This rule is easier to explain if you turn "Show/Hide" hidden formatting ON:

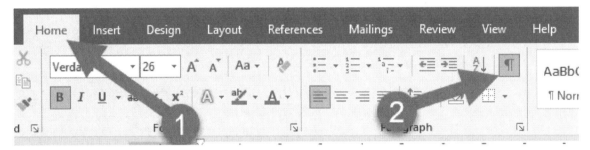

This will show non-printing formatting symbols that are otherwise hidden in the word processor. For example, you should see the pilcrow symbol whenever you press the return (enter) key to move onto the next line:

become more productive and much better organised running their blogs and websites. This tutorial shows how to add a Google scheduling calendar using a simple plugin. The software works with all modern themes and updated versions of WordPress.¶

.Why·Integrate·Online·Calendars·in·WordPress?¶

Here·are·the·main·benefits·of·a·Google·online·calendar:·¶

- → Customisation·options·(no·code·skills·or·tweaks·necessary)¶
- → Display·Google·calendar·at·the·front-end·(site)·as·well·as·the·back-end·(admin)¶
- → Schedule·reminders·and·notifications·for·new·material·and·public·events,·etc.¶
- → Manage·bookings·and·upcoming·appointments¶
- → Responsive·(mobile-friendly)·interface¶
- → Supports·other·authorised·users¶
- → Saves·time·with·improved·efficiency¶

NOTE: The pilcrow symbol may already be visible in your editor without having to turn the visual formatting on.

It is very important to see these characters because they represent hard line breaks.

The rule I want to give you is this:

There should never be hard line breaks on an empty line.

Here is what that looks like:

How·to·embed·your·Google·calendar¶

The·following·steps·assume·you·have·a·Gmail·account·and·know·how·to·install·and·activate· plugins.·If·not,·please·read,·How·to·Install·New·Plugins·in·WordPress·before·continuing.¶

¶

Install·and·activate·the·Simple·Calendar·—·Google·Calendar·Plugin·—·By·Simple·Calendar.¶

From·your·WP·Dashboard,·go·to·**Plugins·=>·Installed·Plugins**.¶

You should only see the hard line-breaks at the end of each paragraph (the pilcrow symbol). If you can see them on their own, between paragraphs, you should delete them. Having hard line breaks between paragraphs will create a very big space between them on Kindle devices. If you have any of these "stranded" symbols throughout your document, remove them.

Just to recap, then, when you are writing a paragraph, finish it, hit the return key ONCE, and then immediately start typing the next paragraph. There will be a visible gap between the two paragraphs in Word, which is added by the formatting we set up for the **Normal** style.

If you follow this rule, you should not get into a mess with the spacing of your documents when they are converted into a Kindle book format. If you know this rule, it should be obvious that you NEVER use the return key (hard line breaks) to space out content.

If you need something to start on a new page (e.g., a new chapter), create a page break

Page Breaks

The correct way to insert a page break in your document is to go to the Insert tab and click the **Page Break** button.

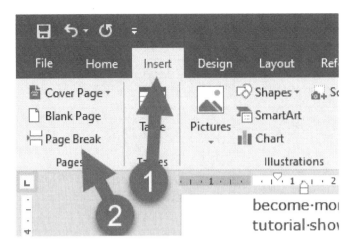

The keyboard shortcut on a PC for a page break is CTRL + Enter key.

If text MUST start on a new page, then insert a page break directly before that text.

For example, use page breaks at the end of a chapter so that the new chapter starts on a fresh page.

Hyperlinks

Most Kindle devices, plus the Kindle reading software on iPads, PCs, Macs, Android devices & iPhones, can read and follow hyperlinks to external websites. If you want to link out to a website, you just create the hyperlink in MS Word by selecting the text you want to use for the link and then right-click on the selected area. You then choose "Link" from the popup menu that appears:

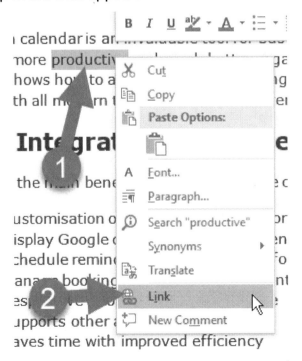

This opens the **Insert Hyperlink dialogue box**:

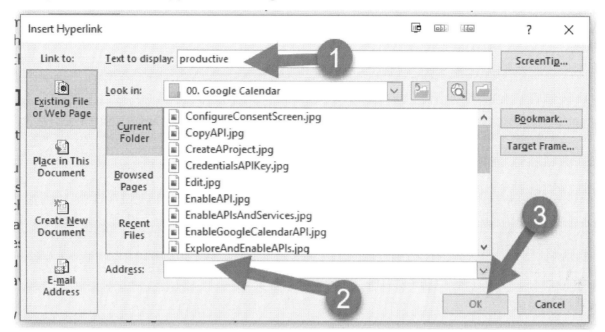

At the top, you can see the text that will be displayed in the link (this is called the link text and will be whatever text you highlighted before invoking the Insert Hyperlink dialogue box), and the address box at the bottom is where you type in the website address you want that text linked to.

Click on the OK button to insert the link into the document.

However, if you intend to create a paperback version of your book, then there is no point in having a link like this.

The reader will see the word underlined (the link) but have no idea where it goes. Therefore, as I have done in this book, if you want to link to a website, use the full URL (or a shortened version).

Lists

When Amazon converts a book to the Kindle format, it sometimes does not display bullet lists correctly. If you have a problem with this when you convert your book, be aware that you can insert bullet symbols manually to make sure you get the formatting you want.

To create a bullet (on a PC), hold down the ALT key while you type in 0149. I believe it is Option 8 on a Mac.

That creates a bullet like this: •

You can then just type bullets manually. Here is a bullet list created this way:

- manual bullet item 1
- manual bullet item 2
- manual bullet item 3

Word's **numbered lists** do convert OK, so you can use those without worry. However, do make sure each new list starts at the correct number (usually 1) and isn't simply continuing numbering where the last list finished. I've had a lot of problems with this, so do be careful to check all numbered lists when you are reviewing your manuscript prior to submission.

Images

Images are important in certain types of books. You can easily add images into your book by inserting them into the Word document where you want them to appear. However, there are a few things to be aware of.

Image format

While there are a lot of different image formats, I recommend you stick to JPG. These tend to produce overall file sizes that are smaller, and therefore less costly to you in download fees.

Specifically, I do not recommend you use PNG files. These can be very large in the final book, so my advice is don't use them.

Image Size

Images take up physical space on a disk drive. The larger the file size, the larger your final Word document will be. Since Amazon charges a download fee on bigger books, you want to keep your Word document size as small as possible. It is, therefore, a good idea to correctly size and compress your images so that they take up less space.

NOTE: If you are using MS Word, it has a built-in feature to compress pictures when you save your document. That means you can create a single Word document with high-resolution images and save it in two formats when publishing. One for the paperback with high-resolution images, and the other for Kindle with lower resolution images. However, you should correctly size your images before you insert them into your document.

First, decide how big your paperback version will be and work out the size of the "content rectangle" that will hold the content of your book. To do that, we need to know page size and margins.

Here is a screenshot of a page from the previous version of this book, with the content rectangle highlighted.

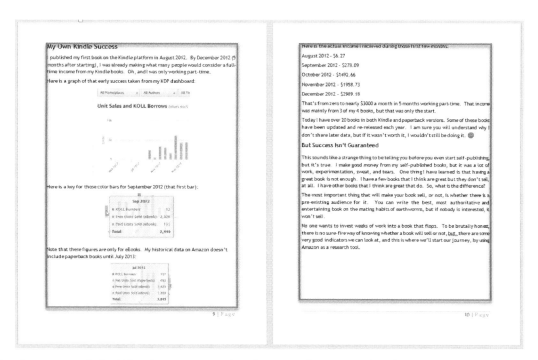

On the Layout tab in Word, you can check your document's size:

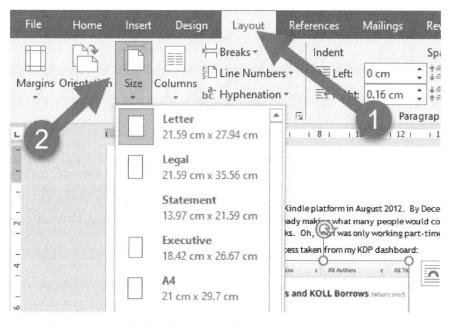

You can see the first entry highlighted to show that this book, my document size is 21.59 cm wide by 27.94 cm tall.

If you need to work in inches

Divide cm by 2.54 to get the dimensions in inches. So, this book is 8.5 x 11 inches.

Alternatively, change the settings for Word in **Options** (via the File Tab), **Advanced** section. Scroll down to the **Display** settings:

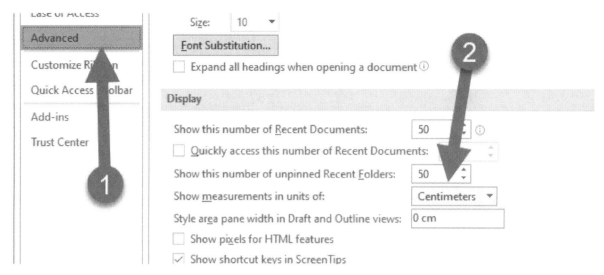

To find the margin, there is a button on the Layout tab which will tell you what you need to know:

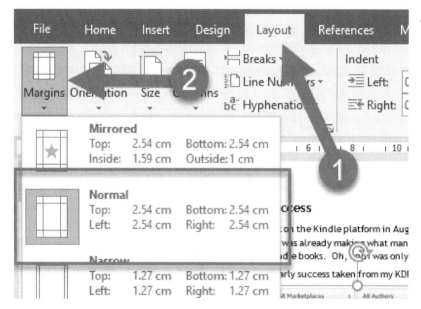

So, my page is 21.59 cm wide, with margins on the left and right of 2.54 cm each. That means the width of my content rectangle is 21.59 cm – 2.54 cm – 2.54 cm = 16.51 cm.

I can work out the height of my content rectangle using the same information. Therefore, the content rectangle of my book is 16.51 cm x 22.86 cm.

With that information, I can correctly size an image before it is inserted into the document. If I want an image to take up the full width of a page, I will resize it so that the width is 16.51 cm in my image editor.

It will then take up the appropriate space in my document:

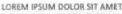

Be aware that if you insert an image that is too small, Word will allow you to stretch it. However, avoid doing this because the resulting image can become very "pixely." Resize the image to the correct size before inserting it, and you'll be fine.

How to Insert an Image

Inserting images can be done in a couple of ways. The first method is to copy the image from your graphics software and paste it into the Word document. I have heard other Kindle authors having problems with this method, but it seems to work fine for me. The other way to insert an image (and most Kindle authors recommend you do it this way) is by clicking on the **Insert** tab of the ribbon bar and then clicking on the **Pictures** button.

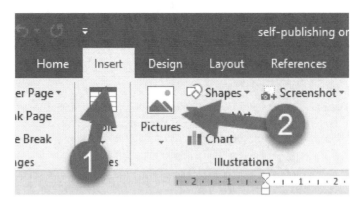

Select **This Device...** from the drop-down menu, and you'll be shown an image selection dialogue box, so choose your image and click the Insert button to insert it into your document.

Color Images v Black & White

I recommend you use black and white images in your Word document.

Some Kindles (as well as tablets & Smartphones) have color displays, and it is nice to have images in color as you read a book. However, traditional Kindles are black and white only, and the Kindle will convert the color image to black and white, often doing a very bad good job. This can make some images look very poor on black and white Kindles. By converting images to black and white before you insert them, you can be sure they look good, and they won't undergo this automatic conversion.

I'd recommend you check your images carefully when you preview your book at the time of upload, just to confirm that all your images look good.

Page Numbers

Kindle devices allow the reader to change the text size of the book they are reading. Because of this, the page you see in Word will not necessarily be a full page on the Kindle device. What you see in your Word document as page 5, for example, may well be page 10 on a Kindle. Therefore we do not include page numbers in the Kindle version of the book.

However, the way we will save the Word document for the Kindle version will strip out page numbers for us if they are in the document. If you intend to publish your book as a paperback, then add page numbers now.

Page Numbering in Word

I like Word, but I also hate it for making things so complicated. Something that should be as easy as adding page numbers to a document is a process that takes a little figuring out.

Step-by-Step Instructions

You might like to add page numbers after you've completed your book, but I am doing it now to highlight an important point that you need to keep an eye on.

Page numbers in a printed book need to start on an odd-numbered page.

As you edit the book, the page you started numbering on may shift around from odd to even and back again. Therefore, you will need to check this before submitting it as a paperback.

Click at the top of the page where you want to start your page numbering. Now check to see what page number it is. In Word, the information is displayed bottom left:

So, the page I want to start numbering on is an even page. That's no good. The easiest way to fix this is to insert a blank page before the one you want to start the numbers on. That will then give me the odd page I need:

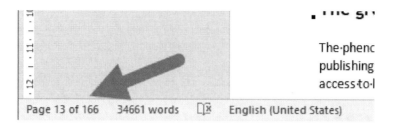

Page 13 of 166   34661 words   🔲x   English (United States)

NOTE: Be aware that we will be adding a table of contents before the numbering starts, so we may need to delete or add blank pages to make sure numbering remains on an odd page.

OK, let's add the page numbers.

Click at the top of the page you want to start numbering on.

On the **Layout** tab of the ribbon bar, click **Breaks** and select **Continuous** from the list:

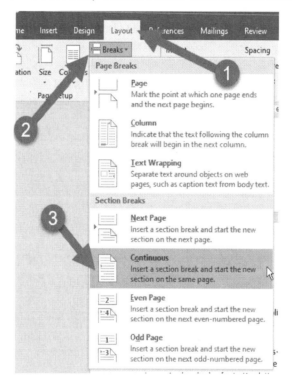

On the **Insert** tab of the ribbon bar, click **Page Number** and move your mouse down to **Bottom of Page**, and select the position and style you want to use.

Word will jump you to the **Design** tab in the ribbon bar. In the **Navigation** section, DESELECT the **Link to Previous** button so that it is no longer highlighted.

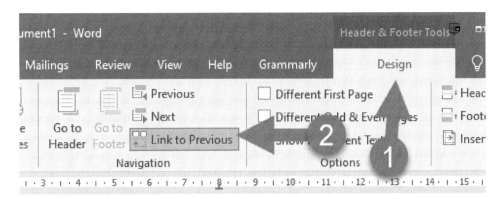

Scroll back in your Word document to the page before your continuous page break, and click into the Footer section of the page to select it:

Now click the **Footer** button in the **Header & Footer** section of the ribbon bar at the top:

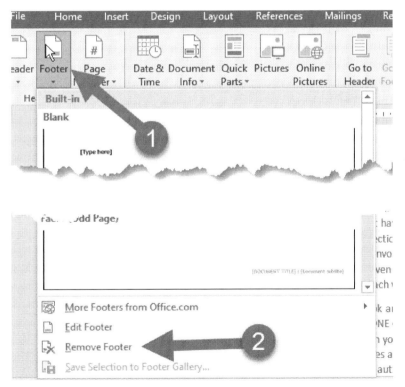

Select **Remove Footer.**

Now click on the **Close Header and Footer** button:

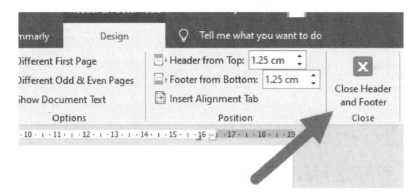

Click again on the page of your document where you want page numbers to begin.

Go back to the **Insert** tab, and click **Page Number, Format Page Number**:

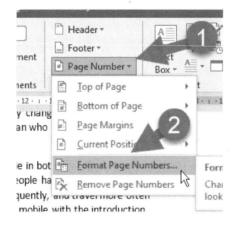

Select **Start at:** and enter 1 in the box.

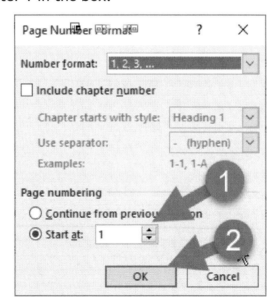

Click OK to save.

Your page numbering should now start at 1, on the page you specified.

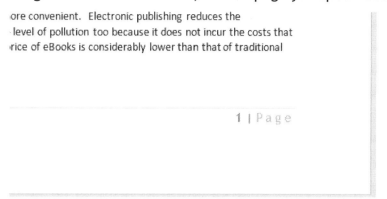

There should be no page numbering on pages before this "first page."

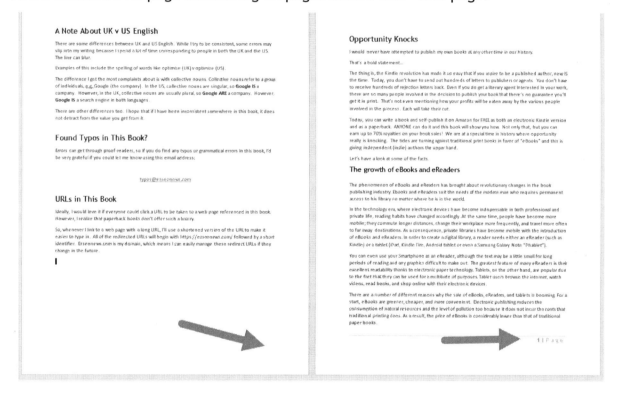

Table of Contents

Your book needs a table of contents, whether you are creating just a Kindle version or a paperback as well.

Let me show you how to insert a table of contents into your book.

Word has a special feature to automatically insert a table of contents (TOC). Scroll to the place in your document where you want the TOC to appear. Make sure this is before the continuous line break that you added for your page numbering. To help locate the line break, click the pilcrow button on the **Home** tab:

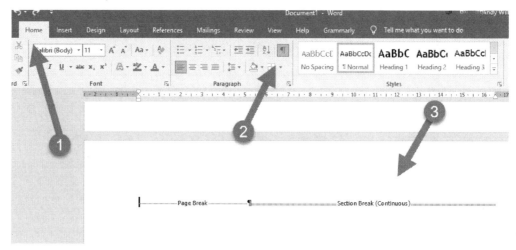

Make sure you click at some point before this continuous break so that your TOC appears on un-numbered pages.

Click on the **References** tab in Word's ribbon bar and then click on the **Table of Contents** button:

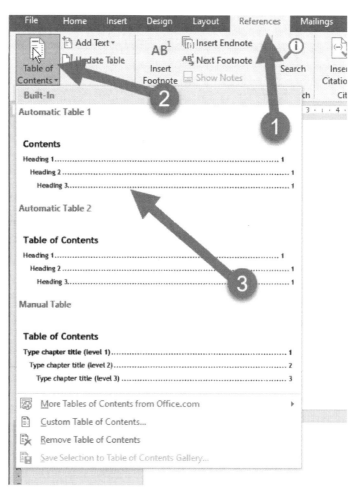

All the "built-in" TOC styles contain page numbers, but that is fine as they will be used by the paperback and stripped out of the Kindle when we save this document in the two separate formats.

Just click on the TOC you want, and it will be inserted into your document.

We now need to insert a bookmark at the start of the TOC so that Kindle devices can "GoTo TOC." This is easy enough.

Move your cursor to the start of the table of contents title (click just before the title starts), and then on the **Insert menu** on the ribbon bar, select **Bookmark**.

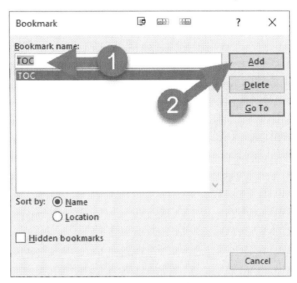

Type TOC as the bookmark name, and then click the **Add** button.

This will add a bookmark that Kindle readers can access.

NOTE: If someone complains that your book does not have this feature, Kindle may remove your book from the marketplace until you add it, so it's important to do it now.

After the last entry in your TOC, insert a page break. This ensures that the next section of your book does not begin on the same page as the final entries of your TOC.

It's a good time to check whether your page numbering still starts on an odd page. If not, then fix that by deleting the page you added earlier or adding a new blank page before it. Be careful not to interfere with the Section Break you added earlier, or it could mess up that page numbering.

Updating a TOC

As you work on your book, you may add new sections or arrange and delete other parts. You'll probably want to update the table of contents as you go along. This is very easy.

Right-click any entry in the TOC and select **Update Field** from the menu.

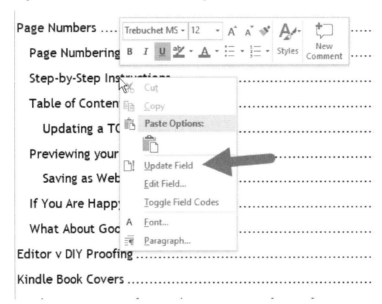

A dialogue box sometimes appears with two options:

You can either update the whole table or just the page numbers. If you've added and deleted sections in your book, update the whole table to be sure they are inserted into the TOC.

Previewing your Book

I don't usually preview my kindle books until I actually submit them to Amazon. During the submission process, you get the chance to preview your book.

However, you may want to preview your book before you upload it. The free Kindle Previewer software available from Amazon will allow you to do this.

Previewer download URL:

https://ezseonews.com/kindleprev

Download and install it (there are Windows and Mac versions). I'll be showing you the Windows version, so it may look a little different if you are on a Mac.

The Kindle Previewer only works with a few file formats which do not include Word or Open Office native formats. Accepted formats are Mobi, ePub, HTML, and OPF.

The easiest thing to do is to save your book as HTML using Word's **Web Page, Filtered** format. This is the same format we'll use to upload the finished book to Amazon, and I have found that this format is the most reliable.

Saving as Web Page, Filtered

Before doing anything else, save your document in Word's DOC or DOCX format.

With that saved, you can now create the HTML version of the file.

You can do this in Word by selecting **Save As** and selecting a location to save your document.

In the dialogue box that opens, choose the **Web Page, Filtered** option.

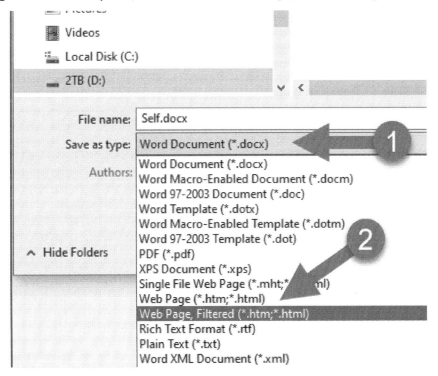

Don't click the Save button yet, as we need to make sure the image size is reduced.

Click on the **Tools** button, and select **Web Options**.

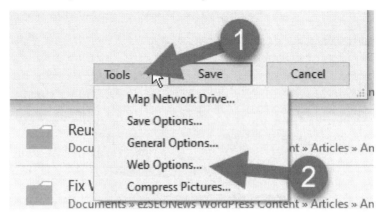

This opens a screen showing web options (web options because we are saving as a web page):

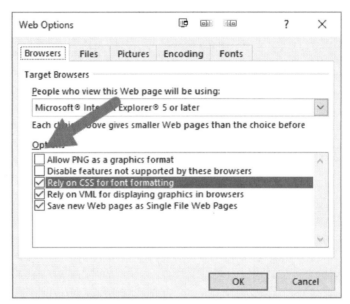

The important option here is the top one. Make sure **Allow PNG as a graphics format** is disabled. Leaving this enabled will cause some images to be saved in a very large PNG format. Remember I recommended not using PNG images? Well, this will make sure that none of your images are converted to PNG when the HTML conversion is made. If you have any PNG files in your document, they won't be embedded in the HTML file.

Once done, click on the OK button, and save your file.

When you do that, the active document in Word will be the newly created web page filtered version of your book.

This will include a .htm document and a folder containing all of your images.

Name		Date modified	Type	Size
Self Publishing 2020_files		29/01/2021 12:47	File folder	
Self Publishing 2020.htm		29/01/2021 12:47	Microsoft Edge H...	335 KB

When you come to submit the book to Amazon, you'll need to zip up the .htm document and image folder into a single zip file. I'll show you how later.

Since we want to load this document into the Kindle Previewer, we first need to close it in Word.

Do that now. Close your Word document.

OK, open the Kindle Previewer software:

Click the **Open Book** link and navigate to where you saved the HTML version of your book.

You'll get a dialogue box saying that your document is being converted. Wait for this to finish, and your book should open in the previewer.

If you get a message saying the conversion failed, check to make sure you closed the copy of your document in the word processor, and try again.

In the top left of the sidebar, you'll see a dropdown box for **Device Type**.

This allows you to change the emulator so that you can see what your book looks like on a tablet, phone, and Kindle E-reader. On the right side of your screen is the book preview.

When you change the **Device Type** setting, the preview will show you how the book looks on that device:

You can navigate through your book by clicking the left/right arrows in this preview screen or clicking directly on the page you want to view:

It is worth going through every page of your document to check that the formatting and general layout looks OK. In particular, check:

Any images you have in your document. Are your images clear? If not, you might want to redo them.

Numbered lists. Do they all start at the correct number?

Bullet lists. Do they look OK with correct alignment?

Blank pages? Remove any pages that are blanks.

Do sections/chapters all start on a new page? If you find any that don't, insert a page break before that title in your Word document.

If You Are Happy, Zip it Up.

When you are happy with your book format, you need to create the zip file that we will upload later to Amazon during the submission process.

When Word saved your document as web page filtered HTML, it saved the main book file as an HTML file in your chosen folder. It also created a folder inside this folder to store all images in your book.

The next step is to zip-up the HTML document and all of the images into a single zip file.

There are a lot of different zip tools available, so I cannot show you exactly how to do this. However, if you have a zip program installed on your computer, such as WinZip or WinRar, then you can create the zip file quickly and easily from Windows File Explorer.

I use WinRar, and the first thing we need to do is select both the HTML file and the folder containing the images.

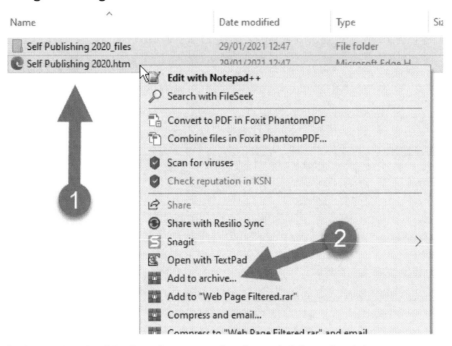

Then right-click on the highlighted pair and select **Add to Archive...**

A dialogue opens to ask for more information on the type of archive you want to create. The only thing to change here is that I want a ZIP file:

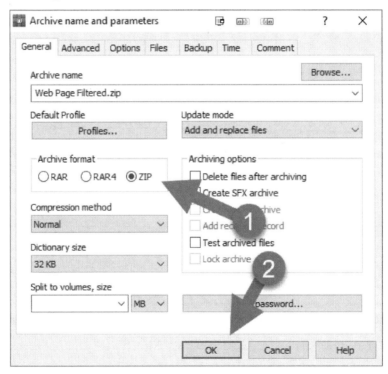

Clicking on OK will create the zip file containing my book.

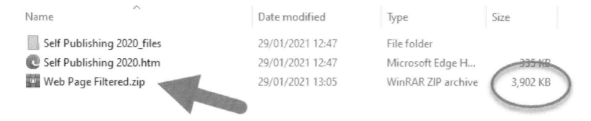

If you open the zip file that you have just created, you should see the HTML file and the folder containing your images. You can also check out the file size of the zip file. Mine is 3.9Mb.

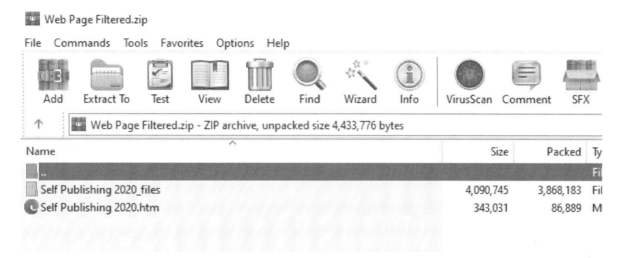

When you submit your book to Amazon, it is this zip file that you'll upload.

Before you go any further, consider the file size of your zip file.

Mine was 3.9 MB in size because of all the images in the book. Since I'll be paying a download fee PER megabyte, it is in my interest to reduce the file size of this book.

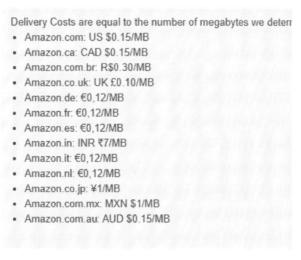

Delivery Costs are equal to the number of megabytes we deterr
- Amazon.com: US $0.15/MB
- Amazon.ca: CAD $0.15/MB
- Amazon.com.br: R$0.30/MB
- Amazon.co.uk: UK £0.10/MB
- Amazon.de: €0,12/MB
- Amazon.fr: €0,12/MB
- Amazon.es: €0,12/MB
- Amazon.in: INR ₹7/MB
- Amazon.it: €0,12/MB
- Amazon.nl: €0,12/MB
- Amazon.co.jp: ¥1/MB
- Amazon.com.mx: MXN $1/MB
- Amazon.com.au: AUD $0.15/MB

If your zip file is really large, check out your images folder that was created when you saved your book as Web Page Filtered. Look to see if there are any really large files you could optimize to make smaller.

What About Google Docs?

Google Docs is a great tool for writers because your books are stored in the cloud. That means you can literally access your work from any computer, or even a tablet or smartphone, from wherever you happen to be at any given time.

To upload a book to Amazon that was written in Google docs, download the book as a web page zip file and then upload that zip file to Amazon.

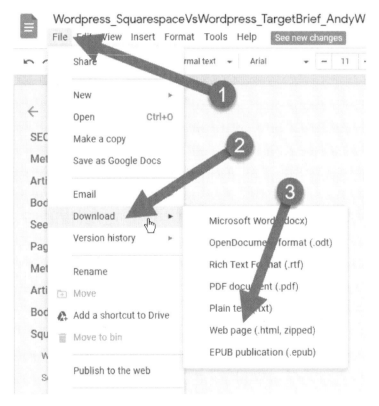

The zipped-up Web document with images will be downloaded to your computer.

Editor v DIY Proofing

Trying to proofread your own book is difficult. You tend to read what should be there rather than what is. In addition, if your own command of language isn't 100%, then you are working on a rocky foundation.

If you can afford it, I highly recommend you hire someone to go through your book and correct spelling and grammar. It doesn't require a full editor, just someone that knows their grammar.

If you cannot afford to hire a professional, then use family and friends. I also recommend you look up Grammarly, or Pro Writing Aid.

Grammarly is an online grammar and spelling service that offers both free and paid accounts. It also has an add-on for Word that can offer suggestions for grammar and spelling, even if you only have a free Grammarly account.

https://ezseonews.com/grammarly

Once installed, Grammarly adds a button to your ribbon bar:

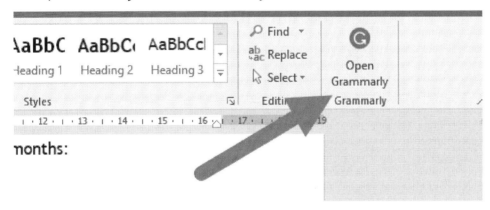

Clicking on that button opens the Grammarly sidebar, which offers suggestions on your Word document:

In this case, Grammarly wants to add a comma before the word "but." It's important to check your text to see whether the suggestion is correct. If it is correct, click on the correction in the Grammarly sidebar to make the change in your Word document.

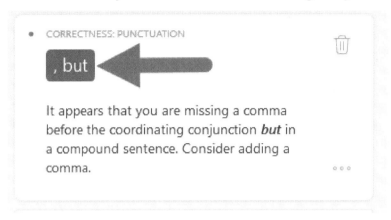

This Grammarly check is something I recommend you do for all your books. Go through your book with this Grammarly plugin to catch the final few errors. I recommend this is the first check you do when you finish writing your book.

Pro Writing Aid is a tool that I have been using more and more.

https://ezseonews.com/prowritingaid

I suggest you check out their site for more details, but once you buy, you'll have a Word plugin to access all the features:

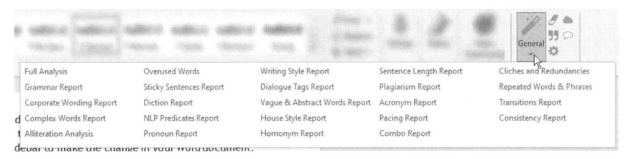

There is also a downloadable Pro Writing Aid editor that can be used to write your book, with real time checking for problems. One of the reasons I like Pro Writing Aid is because it can load and save Scrivener documents, giving you full access to the tools if you use Scrivener to write your books.

Kindle Book Covers

Book covers are the main way Kindle authors get their foot in the door. When someone is searching Amazon, it's the first thing they see. If your cover sucks, people are less likely to click through and read your description or reviews, as they'll assume the book is equally as bad as the cover. Of course, if your cover is bad, you probably won't have many reviews anyway. It is, therefore, VITAL for your success that your covers look professional. Remember, when it comes to selling eBooks, you never get a second chance to make a first impression.

I'd recommend you think of your cover as a headline. You need to use it to get people clicking through to your "sales letter" (the book's product page on Amazon with description and reviews).

Have a look through the Kindle section on Amazon and see what it is that makes some covers appear more professional than others. Look specifically at covers in your niche or genre. Are there any that stand out to you? Why do you like them, what is it that makes them so special? What types of fonts are being used on great looking book covers? What about book covers that look "cheap"? What about colors and layout etc.?

Do they use photos or images? If so, do the images correlate well with the topic of the book? Do the images make you want to click through to the product page?

NOTE: If you want to use a photo on your cover, you need to make sure you have the rights to include the image. The best way to do that is to buy the image license from a stock photo site like iStockPhoto or PhotoDune. I tend to use Photodune as they are cheaper.

iStockPhoto – https://www.istockphoto.com/

PhotoDune - https://photodune.net/

There are some "eBook cover designer" tools that promise to help you make professional-looking covers quickly and easily. I personally don't rate them and think the results look quite poor. A good graphics program is far better if you have a few skills.

Obviously, designing a book cover is beyond the scope of this book. However, if you want to try it yourself, here is a web page that offers good advice:

https://ezseonews.com/design1

Here are a few things to think about:

1. Make sure that the cover looks good in black & white as well as color. Don't forget that older Kindles are B&W, and that is how those readers will see your cover on Amazon.

2. Use professional images (e.g., like photos from the sources mentioned earlier), but *don't use photos that look like typical stock photos* (if that makes sense). If you look through a few stock photos of people, you'll understand what I mean. Also, remember that you don't have to use the full photo (crop it), and you can rotate it vertically to make it "back-to-front." With graphics tools like Paint Shop Pro, Photoshop, or even free tools, you can add effects to these images, so be creative.

3. Use a large, clear font for your title so that it's visible in the thumbnail (in color and black & white).

4. Don't mix fonts on your cover. Choose one (or at most two) that looks good and stick with it. Don't use fancy, curly fonts unless you're in the romance niche, as it can work there, but even then, do check that your title can be read as a thumbnail.

5. Check out Amazon's "Create an eBook Cover" web page for guidance:

https://ezseonews.com/ebookcover

To summarize the main points of that web page, the image should be a .jpeg or .tiff. Dimensions should be a minimum of 625 pixels on its shortest side and 1,000 pixels on the longest side. However, bigger is better, and Amazon recommends 1600 on the shortest side, with 2,560 on the longest side.

6. I recommend you check out your cover as a thumbnail image by shrinking it down so that the longest side of the image is just 250 pixels. Can you read the important text in the thumbnail? This might be the size of the thumbnail being used on Amazon, so you should be able to.

7. Be mindful of the fact that you won't get a second chance to make that first impression.

Where to Get "Professional" Covers Done for You?

Professional covers can work out very expensive. I'm talking about hundreds of dollars here. There are some cheaper alternatives out there, but the cheaper the cover, the more likely you are to be disappointed.

The Cheapest Option

There is a website called Fiverr where you can pay just $5 for a book cover. There are a lot of workers on Fiverr offering this service, but to be honest, most will produce very bad covers. You might strike it lucky, but the general rule of thumb is that you get what you pay for. My biggest worry about using Fiverr for an eBook cover is that the contractor you hire may use images that violate copyright. If that happens, YOU are liable, not the contractor. I'd recommend YOU buy any images that you want to use on your cover and give them to the person designing your cover.

A Little More Expensive

There are a few sites out there that offer pre-made covers you can buy for a reasonable price. Here is a couple:

- https://www.coverkicks.com/
- https://www.goonwrite.com/

Whoever you hire to create your cover, ask them about the copyright on any images they have used on the cover. Ideally, you should ask them about this BEFORE you hire them for the job ;)

Higher Priced Covers

Perhaps one of the best places to get an eBook cover designed for you is on 99 Designs:

https://99designs.co.uk

This site allows you to set up a "competition" to design your cover for as little as £239.

Designers will create designs and offer them for your consideration. You only pay for a design if you use it, and there is no obligation to use any of the designs created.

The good thing is, you can get the design for the paperback book and use the "front cover" of that for the eBook cover. That way to get both covers designed professionally for the one price. Here is a book cover I got designed on 99 Designs:

That is the paperback cover, and with a little editing, I can use the front section of the cover for the Kindle version.

Publishing on Amazon

OK, so you've finished your book, and you have your cover. The next step is to upload your book to Amazon. Fortunately, this is very easy, and all you need is an Amazon account, which I assume you have by now.

We are going to cover both the Kindle and paperback versions, but let's start with the Kindle.

We have already created the web-filtered HTML document and zipped it up, ready for upload.

Uploading your Book to Amazon

Before we look at the process of uploading your book, I want to mention something that is all too easy to forget.

Your book's product page will be its "sales page."

A sales page should help persuade someone to buy, so bear this in mind as you write the book's title and description.

There is one other thing too. A sales page should rank well in the search engines. The important search engine for us is not Google; it's Amazon. We want our book to be found when people search for phrases on Amazon that are relevant to our book. Fortunately, we've got an advantage over most Kindle publishers. Earlier, we found phrases that people were actually searching for on Amazon. Since we know what they are searching for, we know what they want, so we can tailor our sales page to give it to them.

To help our book appear for the terms that people are searching for, it helps if the sales page includes relevant phrases within it.

There are three sections that allow you to enter these keywords when you submit your book – the title, the description, and the search keywords. By using all three areas, we can get a leg-up the ranking ladder.

If you are a fiction writer, chances are you won't want to put keywords into your title, so you'll depend more on the description and search keywords.

If you are a non-fiction writer, you may be able to naturally include keywords in the title.

OK, let's publish.

Head on over to the Kindle Direct Publishing web page - https://kdp.amazon.com

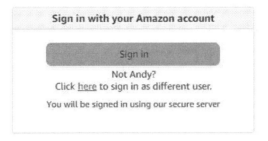

If you don't have an Amazon account, sign up for one from this screen, otherwise **Sign In,** and you'll be taken to your "Bookshelf."

To start the process of adding your new book, click the "**+ Kindle eBook**" button.

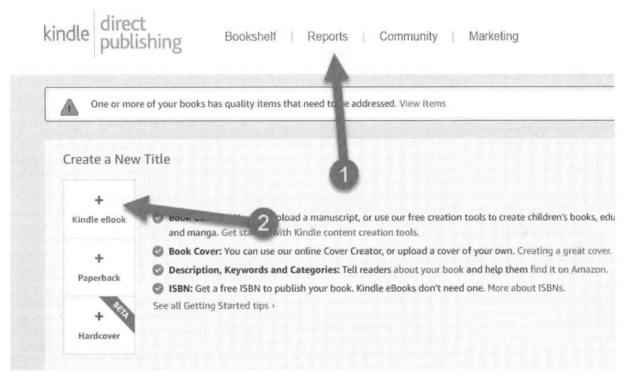

You'll be taken to the Kindle eBook Details form.

The first thing you need to enter is the language for your book, so select the language from the drop-down menu:

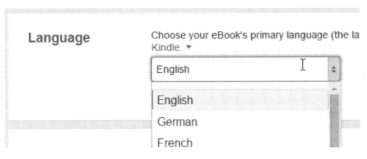

The Book Title

You need to enter the title of your book, and there is space for an optional subtitle:

Book Title

Enter your title as it appears on the book cover. This field canr titles.

Book Title

Self-Publishing on Amazon 2022

Subtitle (Optional)

No Publisher? No Agent? No Problem!

The title of the book is important for two reasons:

1. People will read the title and decide there and then if they want to click through to your product page to read the description and reviews. Does the title convince them that this book is what they are looking for?

2. Keywords in the title will help your book rank on Amazon. Obviously, the higher it ranks when someone searches Amazon, the more chance there is that people will see your book.

Make sure that the title you enter matches the actual title on your book cover. Amazon doesn't want any kind of keyword trickery going on.

For non-fiction writers, the title offers a great opportunity for a little SEO. That is, if you can insert one or two important keywords into the title, your book will be given a ranking boost whenever anyone on Amazon searches for those phrases. However, make sure the title does not look stuffed with phrases as that will put off potential buyers. Make the title read well for humans first and foremost. I like to include the main keywords in the title and then choose something a little catchier for the subtitle.

For fiction authors, you can be more relaxed about your title, but you do need a strong cover. The cover design and title need to tell the visitors on Amazon what your book is about. If you can get their attention, you can get them to click through and read your book description. Obviously, it would also help to get a keyword phrase into the title, but that is far more difficult with fiction. What I suggest you do is ignore the keyword phrases and choose a title that you like and one which will get visitors interested in getting more details about your book. You can still insert the keywords into the description and search keywords section of the submission form.

Is your Book Part of a Series?

This is optional. If your book is part of a series, you can enter a series name and number. For example, a lot of my books are written for webmasters (people that own a website), so I have a "Webmaster" series, with each book (SEO, CSS, WordPress, etc.) being given a different number. Click the button to **Add series details**.

A popup will appear allowing you to create a new series or use an existing one. In my case, the series already exists, so I'll click the **Select series** option. You click the appropriate option and complete the process.

The Edition Number

Next up on the form is the space for an edition number.

The Edition number can help track version changes and is totally optional. It's probably more important for non-fiction writers where books are more likely to be updated over time. The first time you publish the book, you'd give it an Edition number of 1. If you do an update, you can increment that number to 2, and then 3, etc.

Author

Enter your first name and last name in the boxes provided. The author's name should exactly match the name used on your book cover and within the book itself.

If you have a title or letters after your name, you can add these.

A title would go before your first name in the first name box. Letters after your name would be included at the end of your surname in the Last Name box.

Here are two examples:

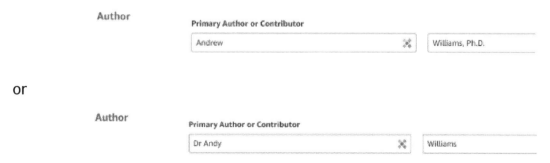

or

A Note About Pen Names

It is OK to use a pen name for your writing. In fact, if you are writing fiction, I'd recommend it so that no one will know your true identity. You'll build up that persona through the channels we'll discuss later in the book.

If, like me, you are writing non-fiction in an area where you have some authority, it makes sense to use your real name.

If there are other contributors to your book that you want to include, you can add these in the next section.

Contributors

This is where you can enter the name(s) of the people that contributed to the book. Other authors, editors, photographers, illustrators, etc. This is optional.

If you want to add contributors, select the type of contribution made, and then add their first and last name.

You can add additional contributors by clicking the Add Another button, which then opens the second row.

You can remove contributors using the Remove button next to the contributor you want to remove.

The Book Description

The next box on the submission form is the book description. The description needs to pre-sell the visitor, and you have 4000 characters to do it.

You should bear in mind that the words you type into your description will help Amazon rank your book in their search results. Remember that list of keywords you collected earlier? Try to get some of them into your description. At the same time, you don't want the description to look unnatural, so make sure you write naturally. If you cannot get a keyword in, then leave it out.

Your description should tell the visitor what the book is about so they can make an informed buying decision, but don't give everything away.

If you are a fiction writer, you want the visitor to be drawn into the story by presenting some of the details but without giving too much away. Try to create an image in their mind that excites them, shocks them, or creates some form of strong emotion. You want to draw them in enough so that they want to find out what happens further in your story.

If you are struggling with this, watch a few movie trailers. Note how the movie producers make the film look exciting but without giving away the full story? This is what you need to do.

For non-fiction books, visitors need two things. Firstly, they need to know whether the book will answer their questions. You, therefore, need to include precise details of what the book covers. The second important point is that the visitor needs to know they can trust you. They need to know that YOU know what you are talking about. If you have specific skills or qualifications related to your book, add that information to the description. If you are an online expert with a website, give the name of that website so they can go and check you out.

In a recent update, Amazon gave us a proper editor for the description. It has formatting options like bold, italics, bullets, and headings. This is a vast improvement over previous methods which involved manually adding HTML code.

Description   Summarize your book. This will be your product description on Amazon, so customers can learn more about your book. How do I format the description? ˅

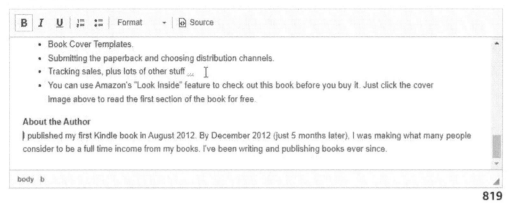

819
remaining characters

Enter your book's description. I usually tweak mine several times before I finally submit my book, so don't worry if you are not happy with your first draft.

Publishing Rights

The next part of the submission form is to verify your publishing rights:

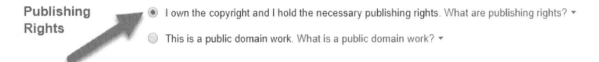

This is where you tell Amazon that your book is either a public domain work, or a book that you wrote (or had written), and therefore own the publishing rights. If you wrote the book, or you had a writer create the book for you, select the first option, "I own the copyright and I hold the necessary publishing rights."

Keywords

Earlier, when we were researching on Amazon, we used the auto-complete feature to find relevant keywords related to our book. We also did a little research on competitor books, so we may have found keywords in their book titles and descriptions. It's now time to put those keywords to good use. You see, Amazon actually wants you to tell them what phrases your book should rank for in their search engine.   You can add **up to** 7 search keywords. Because each search keyword will increase your chances of ranking for that particular phrase, make sure you use up all seven, one per box.

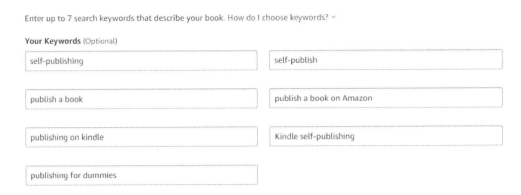

Enter up to 7 search keywords that describe your book. How do I choose keywords? ˅

Your Keywords (Optional)

self-publishing	self-publish
publish a book	publish a book on Amazon
publishing on kindle	Kindle self-publishing
publishing for dummies	

Again, **make sure you use all 7.** These keywords will make a big difference to your rankings on Amazon.

Categories

This section of the submission form allows you to choose the best categories for your book. Every category on Amazon has a bestseller list just for that category. Therefore, it is possible to rank in the top 10 for any category you choose.

You can pick two categories.

Click on the **Set Categories** button to open up the category selection screen:

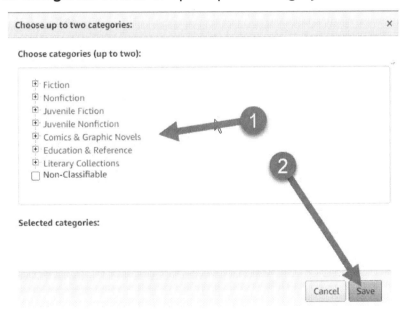

Most of the categories have sub-categories, so you need to expand the relevant section within the category tree to find the two categories that best match your book. When you find the categories, check them off in the list, and you'll see them added to the selected category list:

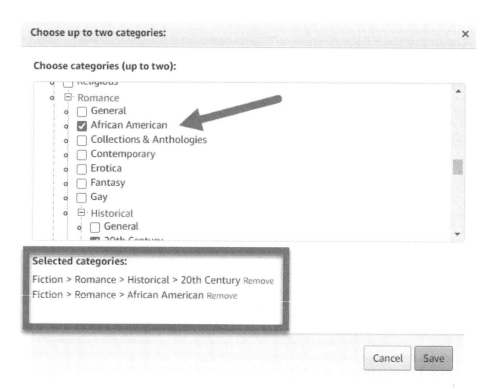

It is better to look for smaller sub-categories and not pick top-level categories like "Romance. Top-level categories will contain huge numbers of books, making it much more difficult for your book to be seen in the category listings. Look for smaller sub-categories inside these top levels. Some sub-categories may have less than ten books, so you'd be pretty much guaranteed a top 10 listing in those categories.

There is something we've mentioned before that is probably very obvious to you now. The categories that Amazon displays on a product page, like these in the Best Sellers Rank section, do not correspond faithfully to the categories you will see when you come to submit your book:

Amazon Best Sellers Rank: #14,485 Paid in Kindle Store (See Top 100 Paid in Kindle Store)
#7 in Kindle Store > Kindle eBooks > Nonfiction > Computers & Internet > Web Site Design
#12 in Books > Computers & Technology > Internet & Web Culture > Blogging & Blogs
#45 in Books > Computers & Technology > Web Development & Design > Web Design

For example, one of the categories above is:

Books > Computers & Technology > Internet & Web Culture > Blogging & Blogs

If you search the category listings while you are submitting your book, you won't find a "Book" category. You also won't find a "Blogging & Blogs" category. This can make things a little more difficult as it means you'll have to go through ALL of the available categories to make sure you find the two most relevant. Choose the best two categories for your book.

TIP: If you want one of your books to appear in a particular category but cannot find anything remotely similar in the Kindle category list, email the KDP support team and ask them what category to select so that the book appears in that category. The KDP help team is there to help YOU, so use them if you need any clarification.

Age and Grade Range

This is optional. If your book is intended for children, then you can select a minimum and maximum age and grade range. Amazon filters books according to these ranges, so if you want Amazon to suggest your book for a particular age or grade range, include that information in the submission form.

Pre-Order

With self-publishing, you have two options. You can publish it straight away, or you can schedule the publication of your book for as much as 90 days in the future. This allows you to collect pre-orders on your book, which will be automatically delivered when it's published.

Be very careful about scheduling your book if it is not yet complete. Amazon does not like publishers that fail to meet their own deadlines.

My advice is to start off by selecting the "I am ready to release my book now" option until you have a little more experience with KDP and understand how pre-orders may be used to your advantage. Be aware that the book won't actually be published until you finish filling out the submission forms, and click the "publish" button.

Once the information on this form is complete, click on the **Save and Continue** button at the bottom. If you want to just save it as a draft to come back to later, there is a button for that too.

If there are any errors or omissions on your form, you will get a notification like this:

Fix the errors and save them again. You should then be taken to the "Kindle eBook Content" section of the form.

The first section of this form asks about Digital Rights Management (DRM):

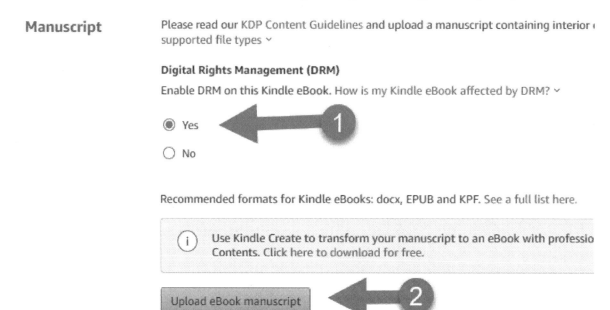

Check the radio button to enable digital rights management. Some people argue that you should not enable this, but I recommend you do it. It makes it more difficult for people to illegally share your book. If you want to know why some people don't mind their books being distributed illegally, do a search on Google for "digital rights management."

You can now click the **Upload eBook Manuscript** button and upload the zip file you created earlier.

Once the upload is complete, you'll see a message like this:

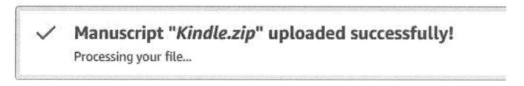

It's now time to upload your eBook Cover.

If you have struggled with the cover, Amazon does offer a basic Cover Creator tool. If you want to check that out, click the button to launch the tool. It is beyond the scope of this book to show you how to use that, but it is relatively intuitive.

If you have a cover to upload, click the **Upload a cover you already have** radio button, and the button to upload your cover will slide into place:

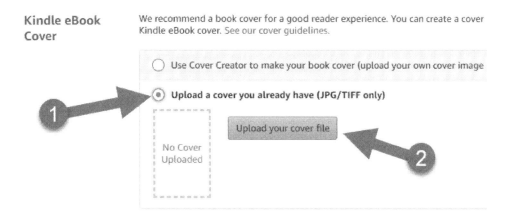

Kindle eBook Cover

We recommend a book cover for a good reader experience. You can create a cover Kindle eBook cover. See our cover guidelines.

○ Use Cover Creator to make your book cover (upload your own cover image

◉ Upload a cover you already have (JPG/TIFF only)

No Cover Uploaded

Upload your cover file

Click the upload button and select it from your hard disk.

On successful completion, should get a confirmation message:

○ Use Cover Creator to make your book cover (upload your own cover image or use KDP's stock images)

◉ Upload a cover you already have (JPG/TIFF only)

No Cover Uploaded

Upload your cover file

✓ **Cover uploaded successfully!**
Processing your file...

Kindle eBook Preview

The next section of this form allows you to preview your book in the online previewer. It can take a little while to convert your book after the cover is uploaded, so be patient.

Kindle eBook Preview

Online Previewer
The Online Previewer is the easiest way to preview. It lets you preview most books as they would appear on Kindle e-readers, tablets and phones.

Launch Previewer

Downloadable Preview Options

ⓘ **We are converting your file. This may take a few minutes. You can download your book after conversion completes.**

If you try to launch the previewer before the conversion is complete, you will probably get an error message. Simply return to the book detail screen and wait a little longer.

The **Launch Previewer** button will show you your book as it will appear on Kindle devices.

You can view your book on simulators for tablet, Kindle device, and phones in both landscape and portrait modes using the toolbar at the top:

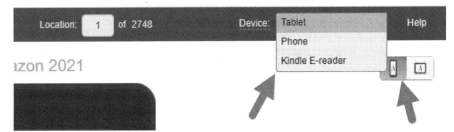

Scroll through your book using the left and right arrows on the sides of the emulator. Check your book, making sure images are all visible. Also, check the formatting of the text, especially bullets and numbered lists. Go through the entire book to check it is perfectly formatted.

Across the top is a drop-down box labeled **Table of Contents**.

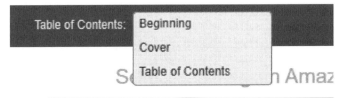

Try out the three options. The third option (Table of Contents) will be there because you added the TOC bookmark to your Word document, remember? If you don't see that entry, go back to your Word document and check it is there.

When you are happy, you can close the previewer by clicking the **Book Details** link at the top left of the page. You can now continue with the submission process.

Kindle eBook ISBN

This is optional as Kindle books do not require an ISBN.

If you want to use one, you can enter it here as well as the name of the publisher (also optional).

Unless you know you want an ISBN for your Kindle book, just leave these boxes empty and click the **Save and Continue** button to be taken to the Pricing screen.

KDP Select Enrollment

The first choice you have is whether to enroll your book into KDP Select for a 90-day period of exclusivity.

For the 90-day period that your book is in KDP, you cannot offer it for sale (or give it away for free) in any other digital format. Joining KDP means that you are making an exclusive agreement with Amazon.

KDP Select means that people can borrow your book for free if they are subscribers of Amazon Prime. For each borrow, you get a fee. The exact fee varies, but I don't want you to worry about this. The benefits of enrolling your book in KDP far outweigh any restrictions imposed on you. Amazon gives KDP Select authors a variety of powerful tools to help you promote your book. Therefore, I suggest you select the "Enroll" option.

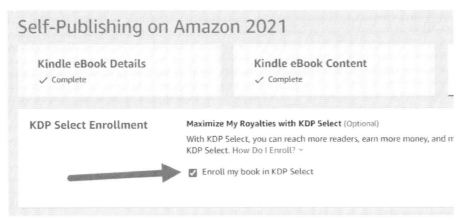

Territories

The next part of the submission form asks which territories you want your book sold in. Unless you have reason to exclude your book from specific territories, I recommend you select All Territories:

Territories	Select the territories for which you hold distribution rights. To enter the Kindle Storyteller conte book available at least in Amazon.co.uk. Learn more about distribution rights.

◉ **All territories (worldwide rights)** What are worldwide rights? ⌄

○ Individual territories What are Individual Territory rights? ⌄

Primary Marketplace

The next option is to choose where you expect most of your sales. Unless you know your book will be mainly sold in one particular country, I recommend you leave this set to Amazon.com.

Royalty & Pricing

This section allows you to set the price of your book on the various Amazon stores, as well as "choose" your royalty rate.

Choosing your Royalty Rate

Pricing, royalty, and distribution

Select a royalty plan and set your Kindle eBook list prices below

○ 35% ◉ 70%

We talked about this earlier. We all want a 70% royalty rate rather than 35%, so if your book is priced between $2.99 and $9.99, select the 70% option.

You can manually choose how much you want to charge for your book in each of the Amazon stores independently, but most people will want to charge the same equivalent value in all Amazon stores. Amazon makes this easy.

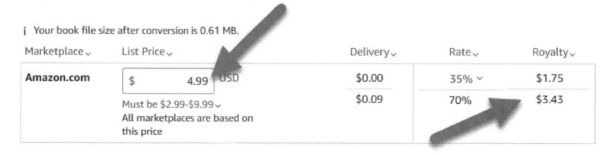

ⓘ Your book file size after conversion is 0.61 MB.

Marketplace⌄	List Price⌄		Delivery⌄	Rate⌄	Royalty⌄
Amazon.com	$ 4.99	USD	$0.00	35% ⌄	$1.75
	Must be $2.99-$9.99⌄ All marketplaces are based on this price		$0.09	70%	$3.43

Enter the price you want in the US Amazon store. Amazon will work out the prices for the "Other Marketplaces."

If you want to sell your book at different "non-equivalent" prices on the various Amazon stores, you can do that too. Just edit the box for that country with the desired fee:

Marketplace	List Price		Delivery	Rate	Royalty
Amazon.com	$ 4.99	USD	$0.00	35%	$1.75
	Must be $2.99-$9.99		$0.09	70%	$3.43
	All marketplaces are based on this price				

The following list prices were converted based on the previous price you entered

Amazon.in	₹ 375	INR	₹318 without IN GST	₹4	70%	₹220
	Must be ₹49-₹10999					
	Based on Amazon.com					
Amazon.co.uk	£ 3.75	GBP		£0.06	70%	£2.58
	Must be £1.77-£9.99					
	Based on Amazon.com					
Amazon.de	€ 4.40	EUR	€4.11 without DE VAT	€0.07	70%	€2.83
	Must be €2.69-€9.99					
	Based on Amazon.com					
Amazon.fr	€ 4.40	EUR	€4.17 without ED VAT	€0.07	70%	€2.87
	Must be €2.69-€9.99					

As you edit the prices, Amazon will update the royalty and delivery columns to tell you how much these are for the new price.

Thoughts on Pricing

Choosing a price for your book is not a simple task. A friend of mine wanted to publish his book on Kindle and told me that he wanted to sell it for $16.99.

I asked him if his ultimate goal was to make as much money from book sales as possible, and he said that it was.

I took out my Smartphone and opened my calculator app. I explained that a Kindle book priced at $16.99 would only be eligible for 35% royalties, that's $5.95 per sale. If he sold his book for $9.99, he'd get 70% royalty, or $6.99 per sale. Not only would he make more profit at $9.99, but he'd probably also make more sales because the price was lower.

NOTE: A lower price is not always a better price.

In my testing, I offered one of my books at $0.99. When I increased the price to $2.99, the sales trebled. It's quite possible that if I increased the price to $4.99, the sales would increase again. Why? It's all to do with perceived value. People do associate price with quality. Something that costs $0.99 is perceived as inferior by many people.

The only way you can find the best price for your books is to test different price points and see what happens to sales. I know this is probably not what you want to hear, but

I can give you a tip.

Look at comparable books in your niche and find some that are written by largely unknown indie publishers. If you don't recognize the author's name, that's fine, just don't compare your book to Dean Koontz or Steven King novels. See how much other relatively unknown indie authors are charging for their book and do your best to price match it. That would be my starting point.

Later, you can start playing with the price to see if you can increase profits. Just remember that it is possible to increase your price, get FEWER sales, and yet still make more profit.

For example:

250 sales a month at $1.99 is $174 profit (remember that this one only qualifies for 35% royalty).

100 sales a month at $2.99 is $209 profit.

80 sales a month at $3.99 is $223 profit.

60 sales a month at $5.99 is $252 profit.

Book Lending

Next on the submission page is a section on book lending. The checkbox for this should be grayed out since you chose the 70% royalty rate.

Book Lending	**Allow Kindle Book Lending** (Optional)
	Allow your customers to lend your Kindle eBook after purchasing it to their days. Learn more about Kindle Book Lending.
	☑ Allow lending for this book Why is this locked? ⌄

All books with a 70% royalty rate are required to be enrolled in Kindle book lending.

Book lending means that people can lend your book to family and friends for a duration of 14 days. You can find out more about book lending by clicking the link in this section of the form.

At the bottom of the submission form is the **Terms & Conditions.**

Terms & Conditions	It can take up to 72 hours for your title to be available for purchase on Amazon.
	By clicking Publish below, I confirm that I have all rights necessary to make the content I am uploading available for marketing, distribution and sale in each territory I have indicated above, and that I am in compliance with the KDP Terms and Conditions.

By clicking the **Publish your Kindle eBook** button at the bottom of the form, you agree to these terms and conditions.

When you are ready to publish your book, click the **Publish Your Kindle eBook** button.

Once the process is complete, Amazon will invite you to start your paperback version. Close that invitation for now, as we will go over the process of publishing the paperback version a little later in this book.

That's it. Your book will take up to 48 hours to be published on Amazon (usually 12-24 hours for books written in English). Once your book is live, you'll be able to see it on Amazon and promote it using the strategies we discuss later in this book.

Amazon will send you an email when it is live.

Updating your Book

If you need to update your book description, categories, pricing, etc., just log into Kindle Direct Publishing again, and you'll be taken to your Bookshelf. All your books will be listed there.

Next to each book is a button on the far right that opens a menu. This gives you access to edit all aspects of your book – details, content, pricing, etc.

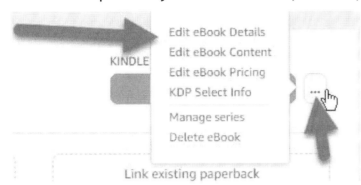

Click the **Edit book details** link to go back to the submission form you filled in when you first submitted the book. The form will be populated with the currently saved data. Change whatever you want (upload a new version of the book, new cover image, change publication date, etc.), and then re-publish. The book will take time to update on Amazon, but the older version will continue to be available for purchase during the interim, so there is no "downtime" in terms of sales (unlike when you update a paperback).

If you want to change the pricing or territories, click the **Edit eBook Pricing** link in that menu. This takes you back to the same pricing & territories screen you saw before so that you can make the necessary changes. Again, it will take a few hours to update on Amazon, so until it does, your book will remain on sale at the original price and in the original territories.

Example

After I submitted one of my books a couple of years ago, I noticed a typo on the opening page:

Promoting your New Kindle Book

Even though you probably don't realize it, we have done quite a lot to promote your book already:

1. The eye-catching cover

2. The high-quality book you've written

3. A great title

4. Choosing the best search keywords

5. Selecting appropriate categories that aren't too saturated with competition

6. Writing an enticing description that uses search keywords where possible.

Without the above in place, any further promotional strategies would pretty much fail in the long-term.

So, with a strong foundation built, what's next?

I'm sure you've read on the internet how you can and should promote your eBooks through social media channels like Facebook & Twitter. You may have even read a book by a best-selling Kindle author who advises you to use Twitter and/or a blog to promote your book(s). Well, I have tested social media, and it really didn't work for me. In fact, talking with other self-publishers about this, social media really hasn't worked that well for any of them, UNLESS they had an established audience to begin with.

The biggest "secret" to promoting your book on Kindle is to:

1. Get a lot of downloads.

2. Get some good reviews & "Likes."

When you do this properly, Amazon actually takes over the promotion of your book, and if it's good, there is a chance that it will take off. We'll look at methods of accomplishing these steps.

From what you have read so far, you may have the impression that I don't use social media in my Kindle promotional strategy. That's not entirely true. In fact, the first thing I recommend you do is set up a presence on Facebook and Twitter. However, this is not so you can blast out book promotions for your first book. It's so those who have read your book can contact and interact with you. Building a loyal fan base is an often-overlooked aspect of marketing on Kindle, but loyal fans are far more than just people who will buy your future books. They are people who will help sell your books to their family & friends, to their Twitter followers, or Facebook contacts. They are people who will ultimately defend you online when trolls come out of the woodwork and take a swipe at you or your work. Don't underestimate the power that even a small number of loyal fans can have on your own success. Make an effort to respond to people who contact you about your work and make it personal. Talk to them as you would with your friends.

In this section of the book, I want to bring the entire promotional strategy together. I'll also discuss a few strategies that you may have heard about from other Kindle authors (some are dangerous to your long-term success and should be avoided at all costs).

The goal of our promotion is simple. **We want to make Amazon sit up and take notice of our book**. Once they do, they'll start promoting the book for you. When that happens, sales can really take off.

Here is a bird's eye view of the strategy we are going to use. You should bear in mind that these things work together so that the sum of the whole is greater than the sum of the individual parts. You should complete all the steps, but don't worry, I'll show you how.

1. You have a high-quality book with an effective cover, title, and description. It should have well-chosen search keywords and two relevant categories that are not too competitive (we want to be able to get into the top 10 for our chosen categories, eventually).

2. You have a Facebook page in your author name so as to keep in contact with readers and bond with them. You can also have a blog if you want one, though a Facebook page is more important early on because of the way status updates on your page will be seen on other Facebook user pages, thus extending your visibility. "Fans" who post on your Facebook page are naturally spreading the word about you and your books to THEIR Facebook "fans." That's how Facebook works and why social channels become very powerful

3. You set up a Twitter account in your author name so people can follow you and keep up-to-date with your releases. This is another channel of contact between you and your readers.

4. You set up an Author Central profile. This is a page on Amazon about you, the author. It can link to an RSS feed on your own site and include images and videos. You can add all your books to this page, so readers can quickly find your books from your profile.

5. You set up a free promotion on Amazon to get as many downloads as possible. During the promotion, you need to "advertise" your promotion around the web. Hopefully, this will lead to your book getting reviews and "Likes."

6. Once reviews come in, you need to use the "Look Inside" feature of your book

to further pre-sell your title.

7. To sell more books, write more books. You should think about serializing your work or creating a "series" where books all target the same audience. This can be done in fiction and non-fiction and will really help sales of all books in the series because, with more books, there is a higher chance your books will be discovered.

We'll go through each of these steps in turn so that you can set this up. We'll also discuss how each of these steps helps in the overall promotion of your book.

Setting Up a Gmail Account

It's always a good idea to separate your book publishing from your private life, so the first thing we are going to do is set up a Gmail account in your author name. You'll use this exclusively for all matters related to your author's name/books. If you eventually publish more books under a different pen name, you should create a new Gmail account for each pen name.

Head on over to Google and search for Gmail. You'll find it listed #1 in Google. Click through to the Gmail website.

Already Own a Gmail Account?

You may already have a Gmail account or two, but the one we are creating now is only to be used for stuff relating to your books.

If you have other Gmail accounts, Google will ask you to log in with one of them. There is no obvious place to click to create a new account. In this case, click on **Use Another Account.**

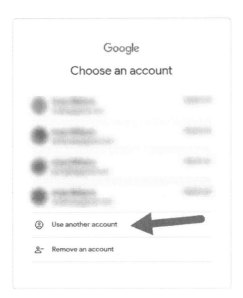

On the next screen, you'll see an option to **Create Account**. Click that and follow the options to create a Gmail account **For Myself**.

Your First Gmail Account?

If this is your first Gmail account, you will see a button to create an account. Click it and go through the process of filling in the form to set up your new Gmail.

You'll be asked to enter a first name, last name, and so on. An important field is the username. You want your author name included here, but chances are it will already be taken. If that is the case, you can add the word "author" after your name, as that is far more likely to be available. e.g., if susandoyle@Gmail.com is taken, try susandoyleauthor@Gmail.com.

Use this email address for everything related to your books.

Step 1 - High-Quality Book & Cover

Already in this book, we have discussed the importance of the book cover, the title, and the description. These all appear on your book product page and can make the difference between sales and no sales. You should have tested your book cover at 250 pixels wide to make sure it is all legible where it needs to be.

These aspects of your book have to look as professional as possible. Also, don't forget that your book needs to be of high quality. If your book is bad, you'll get bad reviews. Negative reviews kill sales, so make your book the best it can be. That way, when the rest of the promotion engine gets going, you'll get sales, which leads to good reviews, which leads to increased sales, which leads to Amazon taking notice. At that point, they'll start promoting your book for you.

Related to this, you chose two categories that were relevant to your book and made sure they weren't too competitive (you stayed out of the top-level categories). You also made use of your seven allocated search keywords. Your product page is now set up and optimized as well as it can be in order to rank in the Amazon search engine and so promote sales of your book.

Step 2 - Facebook Page

We have talked about the importance of having loyal fans. For fans to become loyal to you, there has to be a way for them to contact you. You do have your new Gmail address, but they are unlikely to know that in the beginning. You should set up a Facebook page in your author's name. We'll look at how to do that in a moment.

I'd also suggest that when you have time, you set up a blog in your author's name. Blogs can be set up for free on platforms like blogger.com or wordpress.com, but these blogs do have a number of limitations. I'd, therefore, recommend that when you're able to, you buy your own domain and set up a WordPress blog on that. Teaching you how to set up a WordPress blog is beyond the scope of this book, but I have other books and courses that you can use if you want to learn. Check out the resources section at the end of this book for details.

When you are just starting out, the Facebook page is far more important than the blog, so for now, let's just set up the Facebook page. I'll assume you already have a personal Facebook account (if not, you should sign up for one).

Setting Up a Facebook Page

It's not a great idea to mix business and pleasure on Facebook. Liking and commenting on your granny's apple pie photo one minute, then promoting your new thriller the next, is not a great way to run your publishing business. People interested in your books are not interested in your granny unless, of course, they are family members (or have a craving for apple pie).

The way we get around this is to set up a Facebook Page (not to be confused with your Facebook personal profile). These are totally separate from your personal timeline. Whatever you post on a Facebook page does not get posted on your personal timeline. You can, therefore, keep business and everyday life completely separate.

Think of a Facebook page as a business listing where people can find out details of your business - in this case, you, the author. You need to come up with a suitable name for your Facebook page.

Start off with your author name, exactly as it appears on your book covers. If your cover shows your book was written by John P. Smith, then that should be what you are looking to use on your Facebook page. You want people to easily find you.

If that is taken, then you could use something like John P. Smith Author, John P. Smith Publishing, etc.

By doing this, people searching for you as an author on Facebook would easily spot your page in the search results.

If you are writing a series of books called "Out of Nowhere," you could call your Facebook page "Out of Nowhere." This would make it easy for fans of the series to find your Facebook page on Google.

Facebook & Pennames

For those publishing under a pen name, you may be wondering whether you can just set up a new Facebook personal profile in the author's pen name. In many ways, this would be easier, BUT, Facebook is clamping down on "fake" accounts. No single person should have more than one Facebook account - those are Facebook's rules.

Warning: If Facebook disables your account for not following rules, chances are it will also block you from signing up for another account. Not just for now, but forever. You have been warned.

Of course, you could argue that you and your persona are two separate people, and therefore it's OK. It's a fine line, and only you can make that decision. Personally, I like to make sure that what I do today does not cause me problems further down the line, so I prefer the idea of a Facebook page. Think of these as "business" sections of your Facebook account. You can set up a Facebook page for anything – your favorite band, your website, or your pet cat. You can set up a Facebook page for each of your pen names or each of the book series you write. Facebook pages are an easy way to have a business listing on the web without having to pay for your own website.

Okay, Let's set up the Facebook Page.

I'll assume you have a personal Facebook account already. If not, you'll need to sign up for one. Once you have done that, log in, and we can get started.

Now visit this page:

https://www.facebook.com/pages/creation/

If you are logged in, you'll see this:

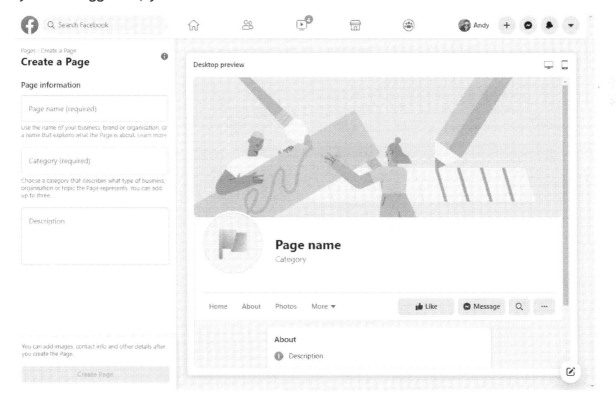

You can enter a name for your page (author name) and a category. Start typing in the category field, and you'll be given some options that match your search:

Author or writer might be good options for the category.

You can then add a description for your page, so think about how you can sell yourself and your books and add that here. You have a 255 character limit.

Once that is all entered, click on the **Create Page** button. You'll then be able to add images, contact information, and other details for your page.

Once complete, you can access the page if you click on the Home button in Facebook, then select Pages in the left sidebar:

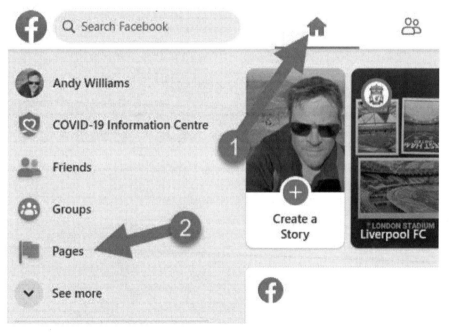

You'll see your new page in a list of all pages you control. By clicking on it, you are taken to that page.

Don't worry about this page being visible for your normal Facebook profile friends. It won't be unless you tell them about it.

You can write status updates on your Facebook page in exactly the same way as you do on your normal, personal Facebook account. You should use status updates to talk about your books or to mention when new releases are coming up and the timing of any free promotions (see later). If you are a non-fiction writer, you can also use it for posting "industry" news.

Step 3 - Twitter Account

Your Twitter account will be used mainly to update followers on the release dates and free promos of future books. Some people will tell you that it is also a great way to get new customers for your books, but I haven't found that myself. I see Twitter as part of my long-term marketing plan as well as a channel through which my "fans" can stay in touch.

Some of your readers will probably contact you through Twitter with direct messages, so always try to respond to them in a timely and professional manner. Remember that we are trying to build a loyal following that will buy, promote, and defend our work for us. Every single person who contacts you is important to your future success, so be nice, and talk to them as you would your friends.

Incidentally, you should always be polite, even to rude people, no matter how hard it is.

Setting Up a Twitter Account for your Author Name

To sign up for Twitter in your author's name, go to twitter.com and click the **Sign up** button.

Fill in your full name, Gmail address (link toggles between email and phone number), and date of birth, then click the **Next** button.

Just go through the sign up screens until you get to the screen with the **Sign Up** button. Click it, and you'll be sent an email with a verification code you need to enter.

On entering the verification code, you'll be asked to create a password. This will then take you into the profile set up, including a profile picture, bio.

At the end of this process, you'll have a working Twitter account. Twitter will assign a username for you, but you can edit this.

On the left of your account is a menu. Select the **More** option at the bottom and select the **settings and privacy** option.

Under the settings column, select **Your Account**, and in the **Your Account** column, select **Account Information**:

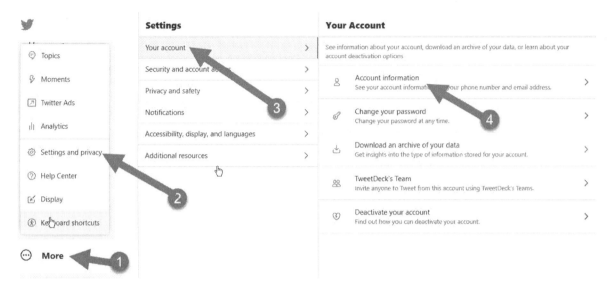

You may be asked to confirm your password, but then you'll have access to account information so you can edit your username:

Change it if you need to.

If You Set Up a Blog

This is totally optional at this stage, but if you do decide on a blog, make sure comments are enabled but require moderation to appear. Also, make sure you have links (icons are better than text links) to your Twitter account and Facebook page so that people arriving at your blog have additional ways to get in touch with you. I'd recommend adding a Facebook and Twitter "button" to your sidebar and have these images link to your Facebook Page and Twitter Profile.

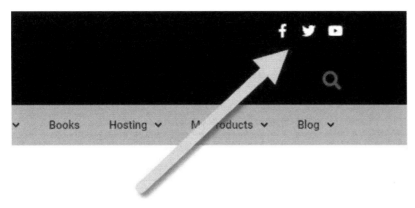

NOTE: You can also have a newsletter subscription form on the sidebar if you want to start collecting subscribers (that you can sell your books to). This requires a separate autoresponder/newsletter service like Aweber, and setting this up is beyond the scope of this book. If you want to sign up for a free trial at Aweber, go to **ezseo.aweber.com** and click the free trial button on the top menu.

Step 4 – Author Central

As soon as your book is published in the Kindle Marketplace, you should set up your author profile in Author Central. Think of this author page as a self-promotion page on Amazon. There will be a biography as well as other information and a link to all your books.

NOTE: There are several Author Central sites catering to authors in different countries. However, recent changes have combined these into a single site. Even though you can still log in at the UK Author Central or the US Author Central, they both take you to the same place. Therefore, go to:

https://author.amazon.com/

Click on the "Join" button:

Fill in your Amazon account username and password to log in. This is the same login you use when you buy stuff on Amazon.

You'll then go through a short setup process.

Once complete, go and log in to Author Central.

You'll be taken to the home page, so click on the **Profile** link in the header:

amazon

Sign-In

If you are a KDP author, sign up or sign in with
your KDP account to speed up account creation.

Email or mobile phone number

Password   Forgot your password?

Sign-In

By continuing, you agree to Amazon's Conditions of

You will be taken to a blank author profile, ready for you to edit.

Add a photo of yourself and a bio. The bio can be quite long but cannot have any HTML formatting.

If you have a blog that you want to be displayed on your author page on Amazon, add that too.

Once complete, you can see what your profile will look like on the various Amazon stores:

Here is mine on Amazon.com:

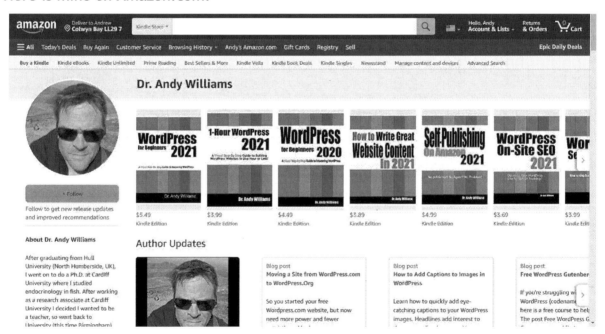

This page contains links to all my books, as well as author updates taken from the RSS feed on my website.

Adding New Books to your Author Profile

Any time you release a new book, you may need to manually add it to your Author Central accounts.

To do this, log into Author Central and click the link to **Books** in the menu bar at the top.

At the bottom of the page, you should see a button to **Add a Book**:

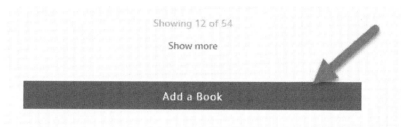

You'll get a search box that allows you to search for your book(s) by title, ISBN, or author. You can also enter the ASIN number contained in the URL of your book's sale page:

https://www.amazon.com/WordPress-Beginners-2021-Step-Step-ebook/dp/B08R44NYLM/ref=sr_1_2?dch

However you search, the results should show your book in the list. Click your cover and then the **Add this book** button on the next screen.

If everything is OK, and it is confirmed that the book is yours, it will be added to your Author Central profile within a few days.

Step 5 – Get Downloads, Reviews & Likes on Amazon

Getting a lot of downloads is the secret to kickstart book sales. What I am about to tell you might go against what your gut tells you but bear with me.

OK, here goes...

I want you to offer your book for FREE for five full days, one after another.

Why five full days?

Because that is what Amazon gives you. When you enroll your book in KDP Select, you are essentially becoming exclusive to Amazon for the next 90 days. In return, Amazon allows you to give your book away for free, for five days within the 90.

OK, so why do we want to give it away for free? I thought the idea was to make money on our books?

Well, it is, but when a book is free, it will get a lot of downloads.

So?

The more "free downloads" your book gets, the more exposure it has. And the more exposure your book gets, the more likely you are to get feedback in the form of reviews on Amazon, messages on Facebook, Twitter, etc., from people that have read it.

Lots of downloads are one of the secret ingredients to a successful book launch on Kindle. Getting reviews is the other. Get these two things, and your book has a great chance of catching Amazon's "eye." This is when their own promotional engine takes over.

Sounds easy, doesn't it? Well, the sad truth is that many people who download your book are unlikely to read it, let alone leave a review. This really is a numbers game. What we need to do is publicize the fact the book will be free, and secondly, ASK for the review.

If you are established in your niche, then you may already have a mailing list that you can use to promote your free download period. If you are just starting out, then you need to find other places where you can promote the book and get it downloaded and hopefully reviewed.

Fortunately, there are a number of websites that will publicize your freebie to their audience, many for free. Some of these sites will want advanced notice of the promotion dates, while others will only want to be notified when the book is available. Do a Google search for **Kindle free promotion,** and you'll find some.

Besides relying on the freebie downloaders, where else can you get reviews?

Friends & family are one option. If you are active on any social media (Facebook, Twitter, Google+, Pinterest, etc.), then that is another option. While I am sure that Amazon doesn't like this type of "friend" review, we do all need a little leg-up when first starting out, so just don't make it too obvious. I recommend you only ask people to leave a review IF they read your book AND they like it.

Consider sending review copies to people that might be interested in your book. Ask them to include a sentence in their review stating that they received a review copy. That will keep Amazon happy.

Ask everyone you know to:

1. Write an objective review and not just a "Great book" with 5 stars. If they think the book deserves a 5 star, then great, but don't forget that a 4 star is still a great score! At this point, getting four or five good reviews is critical.

2. If they enjoyed the book, ask them to mention it to their friends, tweet it on Twitter, and/or post on Facebook, etc.

Setting Up the Free Promotion on Amazon

I'll explain the full promotion schedule in a moment, but first, let me show you how to set up the free promotion on Amazon.

1. Log into KDP.

2. On the Bookshelf tab, click the **Promote and Advertise** button next to the book you want to promote.

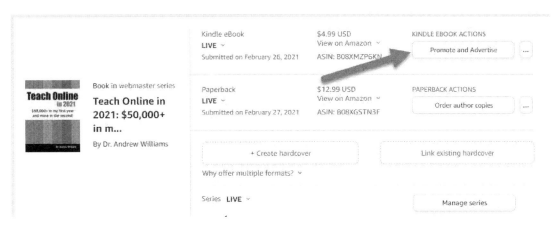

The screen that loads will show your KDP Select status at the top. It will tell you when you enrolled in KDP and when your 90-day exclusivity period finishes. If you decide you want to take your book out of KDP, you can click the **Manage KDP Select Enrollment** button and uncheck the box to automatically renew it into the KDP Select program.

You will see a section on this page called **Run a Price Promotion**.

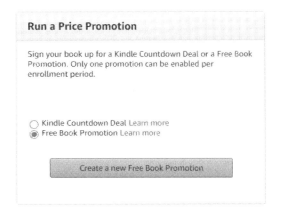

Select **Free Book Promotion** and click the **Create a new Free Book Promotion** button.

The screen that opens allows you to choose a starting date and end date.

A lot of sites where you can promote your free book giveaway require a little notice, often 5 – 7 days. Therefore, if you intend to notify any websites about your giveaway, it is best to schedule your giveaway for a week into the future to give yourself time.

Enter your start and end date and click the **Save Changes** button. You will now see your promotion has been set up:

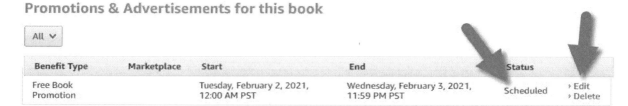

Notice that you can edit or delete the promotion if you change your mind, but don't leave it until the last minute.

OK, now we know how to set up a free promotion, let's look at the promotion schedule.

Free Promotion Schedule

Here are the steps for scheduling the free promotion:

1. Choose a date for your promotion. I personally include a weekend within the 5 days of my promotion, as weekends have performed better for me than weekdays. However, I have heard other people say the opposite. You may need to test this yourself to find the best days for your own promotions, as I am sure it may depend on the type of book. Personally, I'd start a free promotion on a Thursday or Friday and leave it running for 5 days straight. Set up the free promotion on Amazon.

2. **At least 7 days before the promotion:** If you already have your book published and therefore know the Amazon URL or ASIN number, submit your book to the free promotional sites that require several days' notice. You'll know the dates of your free promotion.

3. On **day one** of your promotion, contact the free promotional sites that only accept submissions for books that are currently free. Submit your book to these sites.

4. Leave the promo running. After the 5 days are up, your book will automatically revert to the paid version on Amazon.

At any time during this process, you can get some reviews. As soon as you get a couple of positive reviews for your book, move onto the "Look Inside" feature (below).

Lists of Sites that Can Promote your Book

There are a lot of websites out there that allow you to submit your book when it is on a free promotion. These sites then promote your book to their own visitors, so your book can potentially get a lot of exposure.

The list of websites promoting free book giveaways is constantly changing (some disappearing, new ones appearing). Therefore, I recommend you search Google for **free eBook promotions** and start creating your own list of preferred submission sites.

Remember, some sites will require notice; others require that your book is free at the time of submission, so bear that in mind as you schedule your promotion.

Using Computer Software to Automate Promotions

Creating a free giveaway can be a lot of work when you need to promote your free giveaway to a lot of websites. There is one tool that I use to help with this, called KDROI. It's a web browser extension that works on PC & Mac in Chrome or Firefox.

https://ezseonews.com/kdroi

Let me show you how a free promotion would work with this tool.

The first thing you need to do is schedule a free giveaway. Most sites require several days' notice, so make your first promotion at least 7 days from now.

After installing the KDROI extension in your browser, you'll see this icon:

Go to the Kindle page on Amazon that sells your book, and then click the KDROI button. The KDROI dialogue box opens:

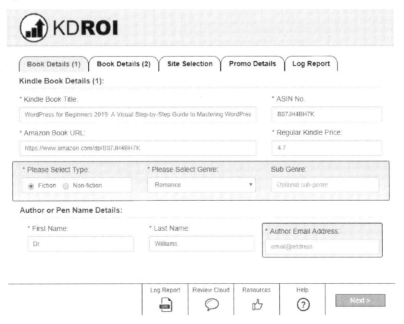

This extension will try to auto-fill a lot of the information from the sales page, but check:

Title

ASIN

Book URL

Regular Price

Fiction / Non-Fiction radio button and genre if appropriate.

First & Last Name

Author email address

Be aware that the email address you enter will be used by the sites you submit to, and you might need to confirm a link in an email they send you before your free advert appears on their site. I would advise you to set up a throw-away Gmail account for the purpose of freebie submissions, so you don't end up getting spammed by these sites.

When these are all correct, click the **Next** button.

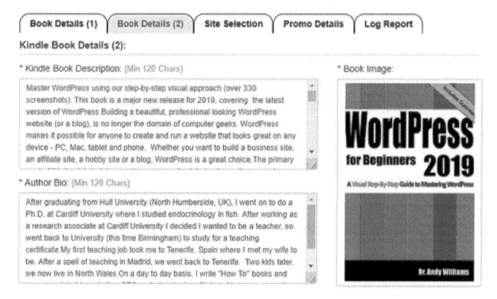

On the second screen, you need to enter your book description and bio. These can be copied directly from the Amazon sales page. You also need to select the book cover image. I think these items should be auto-filled, but on my copy, they aren't.

With description, bio, and cover correct, click **Next**.

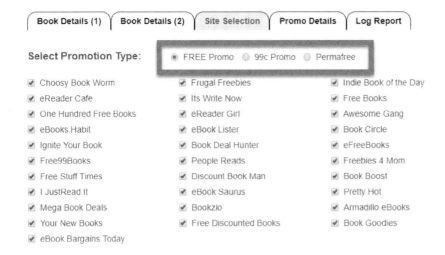

On the **Site Selection** screen, you can choose between free promo, 99c promo, and Permafree promotions. We are only going to look at the free promo, but be aware that you can promote your books on 99c sale or Permafree, too, using this tool. The list of sites that your book will be promoted to will depend on what you choose for promotion type. Not all sites accept all types of promotions.

Although this can change with software, the free promotion of books is currently promoted to around 30 sites. That means your free promo can be seen by visitors and subscribers to those 30 sites.

OK, when you are ready, click on the **Next** button to select your free promotion days:

Make doubly sure your promotion dates are the same as the free promotion you set up on Amazon. When ready, click the **Submit Promotion** button.

You'll be able to follow the progress of the submission and see failures.

#	Kindle Book Title	Author Name	Promo Start	Promo End	Submissions	Status
1	WordPress for Beginners 2019: A Visual Step-by-Step Guide to Mastering WordPress (Webmaster Series Book 2)	Andy Williams	2018-10-29	2018-10-31	19(12 Failure)	Successful

(Tabs above table: Book Details (1) | Book Details (2) | Site Selection | Promo Details | Log Report)

You can see that my submission was successful at 19 of the 31 sites but failed at 12 sites. If you click the blue success/failure link, you'll get to see which submissions were successful and which failed.

While a success rate of 61% may not sound great, that's 19 sites that will be promoting my free giveaway for me, all with just 5 minutes of work.

Now, before you do anything else, check your emails to see whether any of those sites have requested you to click a link to activate your promotion.

If you want more information about this tool, check it out here:

https://ezseonews.com/kdroi

If you have a list of your own, also send out an email to that list on the morning your promotion starts.

Kindle Countdown Deals

Amazon also allows KDP Select books to use **Kindle Countdown Deals**. The idea here is to allow publishers to offer their books at a discount for a limited time, with a visible countdown timer.

Whether this is something you want to use probably depends on your own situation. For example, this is something I would use (instead of a free promotion) when book sales started to decrease. It is also something I would use if I released a major update on my book, just to bring it back to the attention of potential buyers.

The advantages of the Kindle Countdown include:

1. You can control how long your book is on special offer, and those visiting your book sales page will see the time remaining for the special offer pricing before it returns to its normal price.

2. You can offer your book below $2.99 during a Kindle Countdown and still qualify for 70% commission if your book normally gets a 70% commission.

3. Amazon has a Kindle Countdown Deals page, (www.amazon.com/Kindlecountdowndeals) where offers are shown. While you will be competing against a lot of other people for a slot at the top, this

chart will offer extra exposure for your book.

4. KDP has a report to monitor sales and royalties in real-time at each price, discounted or pre-promotion, to help you monitor your results.

In reality, I have never found Kindle Countdown deals to be very effective. That might just be my own books, so you might want to test this for yourself.

Step 6 - The "Look Inside" Feature

As soon as you have received a couple of good reviews for your book, work on the "Look Inside" feature. When I added this feature to my first Kindle eBook, sales increased between 50-70%! Since then, I've added it to all of my books ASAP.

So, what is this feature?

For Kindle books, Amazon has a "Look Inside" feature that allows visitors to the Amazon website to look inside the book. Needless to say, this helps people to decide whether they want to buy it or not.

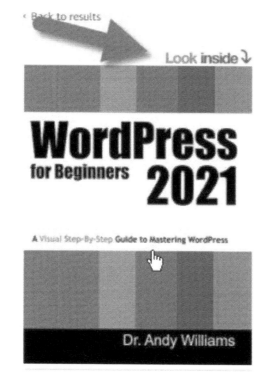

Visitors on Amazon can simply click the book cover to see inside.

Amazon will show the first 10% of the book's content. Knowing that we can use it to our advantage to help promote the book.

Go through the comments that people have left for your book, and pull out any quotes that praise you or your book. Get as many as you can (and don't forget to add more as you get additional reviews in the future).

Now, create a section at the start of your book (I recommend adding it before the table of contents if you have one):

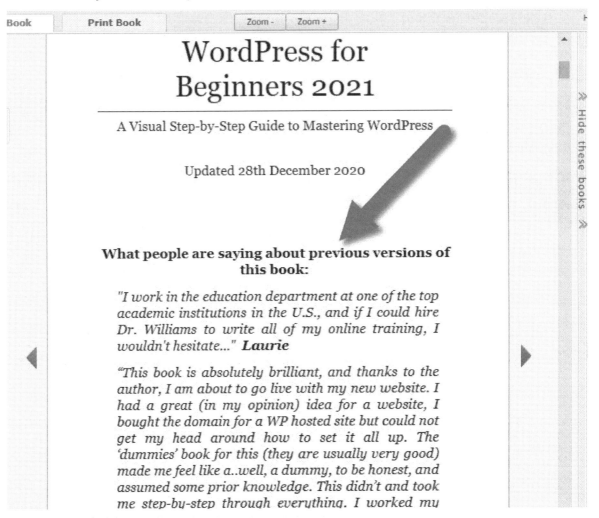

Over time, add all of the positive comments that people are saying about you or your book, and make sure you include the name of the reviewer.

If you are a fiction writer and have several books on sale, you could create a "What people are saying about John Blackstone" section instead. This would be different in that the comments are about you, the author, and not about that particular book. The advantage here is that you have a readymade "What people are saying..." section for any new book you release without having to wait for reviews on the new book itself. This is what John Locke does.

I'd also include links to your Facebook and Twitter pages within the first 10% of your book. If you have a blog set up, add that as well. By doing this, even if someone decides not to buy the book, they still know where they can contact or follow you.

A Note for Fiction Writers

You'll probably want to make sure that enough of your story is found in the first 10% so that potential customers will be able to read enough of the book to get them hooked. I'd also make sure there is a "What people are saying.." section, but this will be a balancing act between how much story and how many testimonials are included in the Look Inside feature.

For non-fiction writers, I personally don't worry too much about how much of the book content is included in the first 10%. As long as you include a "What people are saying section" and a table of contents, then people know what they are getting.

OK, that's the main promotional strategy for your first book. However, as you move forward as an author, there is one thing you can do to sell more books. Write more books! This is where we should discuss serialization, which is extremely powerful for boosting sales.

Step 7 - Serialization of your Books

What do I mean by serialization? Well, it's a number of related books, sold as a series. For example, I could set up a "Webmaster Series" of books and include my SEO book, WordPress book, and CSS book. They are all related and therefore might be of interest to someone who bought one of the other two.

For fiction writers, it's a similar concept. It's a set of books that are related to one another. This relationship might be:

1. One book follows on from another so that the "whole" story is split up into separate books. We'll see the same main characters appear in each book (unless they are killed off!). A good example of this is the Harry Potter series.

2. The main character flows through all the books, but individual stories are not related to each other. An example here could be John Locke's Donovan Creed series. Each book in that series is a completely separate story, but the main character is one and the same.

So why create a series?

Well, there are several reasons:

1. People who like one book in the series are likely to buy the next. If your series is good, you'll build up a loyal fan base, which, as we mentioned earlier, is one of our main goals as indie publishers.

2. You can give away the first book in a series to get readers hooked on the story. If they like it, they'll buy the other books in that series. The more books they read, the more likely they'll become a loyal fan and a paying customer of your

other works.

3. Each book in a series, where the story is continued from one to the next, will leave the reader wanting to buy the next one to find out what happens.

4. The more books you have out there, the more likely it is that someone will find your work and become a paying customer.

5. You can package up a series into a larger product and sell it at a discounted price when compared to the cost of buying each book in the series individually. Faced with saving money, many people will buy the series "bundle," saving themselves a few bucks in the process. Many people who do buy the bundle would not have bought all the books in the series anyway. The other good thing about bundles is that they build fan loyalty because your buyers get to see that you offer more value for money.

A popular trend over the last couple of years is for new indie publishers to write a book and split it into three parts, releasing it as three separate "novellas." The first book ends on a cliff-hanger, encouraging the reader to buy the second one and so on.

These "novellas" are priced at the lower range, so readers don't mind this. However, where many indie publishers go wrong is that they release part 1 and wait to see what sales are like. They will eventually see sales die off, and this kills motivation. Chances are they'll decide that it's not worth spending the time and effort to write part 2 or part 3. This leaves readers feeling cheated. This scenario is actually quite common.

Compare that to what might happen if you wrote all three parts before releasing the first one.

When someone finishes the first book, the second one is available. When they finish that one, the next is available. Anyone who gets to the end of the third book is likely to be a loyal fan by then, and that means they are now part of your promotional army – buying, promoting (telling friends & family), and defending your reputation against trolls. That's a completely different type of reader to the first scenario.

In 2012, when I was looking for inspiration to start publishing on Kindle, I read a novella by a fellow Internet Marketer. Let's call it book 1, series 1, as the author planned it as a 3-part story. I read the book in an afternoon and really enjoyed it. I would have bought the second book if it had been available, but it wasn't. In fact, the second book never materialized. If she ever does release parts 2 and 3, I won't be buying them as I have moved on. She lost me as a reader.

Think about what this has done to her reputation as a writer. Maybe she gets a new idea for a series (let's call this series 2) and is so excited by the idea that she writes book 1 in series 2 before completing series 1. How many people who bought book 1 of series 1 would buy book 1 of series 2? Probably not very many because they wouldn't have much faith that the story would ever get finished.

I can see why this author lost interest in her project. From her point of view, she would have seen a good spike in sales with her Amazon Best Seller's Rank hitting the top 5,000 or higher for a while. She *was* making good daily sales. However, as the weeks passed by, the Seller's Rank dropped, meaning she wasn't making daily sales. What motivation did she now have to continue with that story?

Had she written all three books in the series and released them shortly after one another, sales of each novella would have helped drive the sales of the others. She could also move onto a new project knowing she had fans that would probably buy & promote her next book and defend her reputation.

Whatever type of books you write, consider the added benefits of writing serialized books. This really is one of the more powerful marketing strategies, especially for the fiction writer. Just be clever with it. If you plan a 3-book series, don't release book 1 before book 2 is complete, or at least nearly finished. And make sure book 3 is ready to be released soon afterward. As I mentioned earlier, an ideal situation would be to have all three books ready (or at least the first draft) BEFORE releasing the first one.

What Not to Do When Promoting your Book

I have read a number of blog posts and books on Kindle publishing. Some give good advice, whereas others offer VERY bad advice. You need to remember that Kindle is Amazon's business. If Amazon thinks you are abusing its system, it can and will shut you down. Are you prepared to take that risk?

I thought not.

Here is a list of things I strongly advise you NOT to do.

1. **Do not buy reviews**. Bestselling Kindle author John Locke has admitted to buying reviews. You can read the full story here: https://ezseonews.com/reviewstory
   Some people think that buying reviews is no worse than giving your book away and asking for a review. The reviewer is getting something in return for their review. I personally don't see a problem with asking people to review your book IF they like it, even though it was a free download. However, paying people to leave reviews is clearly not what Amazon wants for its review system. That also goes for paying people to leave bad reviews on your competitor's products. It does happen, but my advice to you is DON'T do it.

2. **Do not create fake Amazon accounts** and leave reviews yourself. I have seen this many times, and it's usually quite obvious. Lots of reviewers, usually without photos, only ever reviewing the one product, or a range (or series), of

products by the same author.

3. **Do not hijack other people's product pages** with reviews that have links to your own book. This is another tactic that I have read about, and it's a tactic that one author teaches in his popular Kindle book. Again, this is a clear tactic to try and manipulate the rankings system. Amazon is deleting reviews that they think are bogus, and this type of review screams fake. Don't get other people to leave this type of review either.

How Facebook Page & Twitter Fit into your Promotional Strategy

Your Twitter and Facebook accounts will become more valuable to you as you become better known for your books. You'll be able to use those accounts (and that blog you'll eventually set up) to announce free promo days and any new books. However, don't think that these accounts are something you should leave until "later." Set them up NOW, because people who read your first book can and will contact you through Twitter and Facebook.

Teaching you how to use Facebook and Twitter is beyond the scope of this book, but there are some great free tutorials online that can help you out. Do a YouTube search for help.

Using YouTube to Promote your Books

If you have the skills required to create videos for YouTube, then you have an advantage. YouTube can give you a lot of free exposure.

Since YouTube is owned by Google, videos tend to rank well on the Google search engine. If you are a fiction writer, you'll need to think creatively about how you could use YouTube to promote your books. Non-fiction writers have it a little easier, as you can just create small tutorials that then link to your book.

In your YouTube video description, you can include a link to your book.

Setting Up Tracking Links

It's interesting to know whether links under your videos are being clicked. This isn't only valuable for links you place in YouTube video descriptions. If you write an article, submit it to another site, and include a link to your book in the article, wouldn't it be nice to know how much traffic that link is sending you? If you know a particular site is a good source of traffic, you can use that site more often.

The plugin I have always used for tracking my links is called Pretty Link (for WordPress).

This plugin allows you to create trackable links that are a lot more visitor friendly. For example, instead of this:

https://www.amazon.com/dp/B07MCR7HRR?&linkCode=ll1&tag=myID-20&linkId=c1cddbe9a9ae6bb196a3d029960e7444&language=en_US&ref_=as_li_ss_tl

You'd get something like this on your own domain:

https://ezseonews.com/SEO21

Try that URL in your browser and see the URL you end up at.

When a pretty link is used in the YouTube description, it will redirect the visitor to the Amazon product page for the book. You'll also know that one visitor came to your book through that YouTube video. By setting up tracking links for different promotions, you can see which promotions are working and which aren't

See how valuable this can be?

Pretty Link Disadvantage

As useful as tracking is, there is one big downside to using tracking plugins. These plugins will cloak your links, and a feature on Amazon that I recommend you use, won't work.

I recommend you join the Amazon affiliate link and create all links to your book from within that program. This is not to make commissions on your books, as you'll make the money from the sale anyway. This is about a feature called One Link.

If you join the Amazon affiliate program and create a link to your book, that link will auto-redirect a person to their local Amazon store. If someone clicks your link in Australia, they are directed to the Australian Amazon site. Someone in the UK will be directed to the UK site, and so on. When you cloak an Amazon affiliate link, this redirection doesn't work so you lose the benefit.

Before Amazon created One Link, Pretty Link was a no-brainer. However, the advantages of auto-redirects are very important.

There is a solution. The paid version of Pretty Links allows you to set up geographic redirects, so that you can create a single, tracked link that will redirect to URLs you specify. You can find out more about this on the Pretty Link site here:

https://prettylinks.com/docs/geographic-redirects/

You grab a link for your book from each of the Amazon marketplaces and set up a Pretty link that will auto-redirect depending on where you visitor is coming from. It's the best of both worlds, though unfortunately works out quite expensive with an annual subscription to the plugin. You may be able to find free or cheaper WordPress plugins that can do the same thing.

Permafree Books

If you are just starting out as a fiction author, it can be hard. It's easy enough to publish your books, but it's just not as easy to get people to buy them from an unknown author. One of the best strategies for new fiction authors is to create a Permafree book that will give you a better chance of bringing in new readers.

It is essentially a book that will always be free (bear with me), therefore encouraging the download. By offering the book for free, you take away the "risk" to the reader so that they can "try before they buy" your other books. The Permafree book should be a taster of what you have on offer and will naturally lead to one or more paid books.

e.g., You may create a Permafree short story, which is the "prelude" to the main novel, or series of books (see later if it is a series). People download the free short story, like it, so go on to buy the novel that the short story introduces them to.

Now the catch.

Amazon doesn't allow you to create permanently free books. Sure, you can give your book away for up to 5 days in every 90 if you are in KDP Select, but that doesn't help much. To get Amazon to show the book as permanently free, we need to use a loophole. That loophole is price matching. If your book is available for free on another platform, then when Amazon finds out about it, they will price match (making it what we call "Permafree."

Steps to Permafree

1. Take your book out of KDP Select:

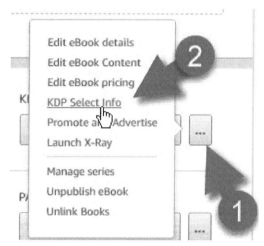

You'll need to uncheck the automatic renewal and save:

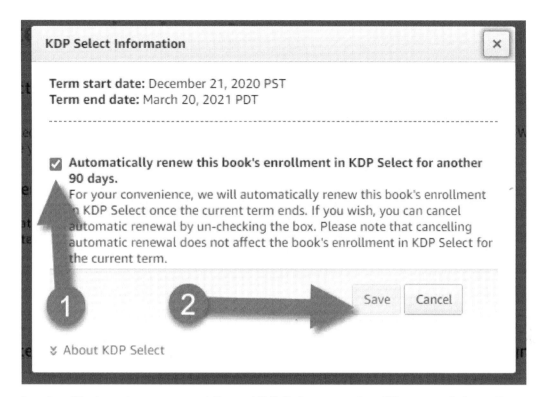

Your book will then be removed from KDP Select on the "Term end date."

2. Upload your book to another retailer, like iTunes, Kobo, Barnes & Noble, Scribd, or Smashwords. Make the book $0.00 on these other retailers.

3. Once your book is published for free elsewhere, you need to request a price match with KDP support by going to the **Contact Us** page here:

https://kdp.amazon.com/contact-us

Click the **Price Matching** link in the **Pricing** section and follow instructions to send your request.

Getting your book changed to free is "at the discretion" of Amazon. However, it should happen within a few days of letting them know. If, after a couple of weeks, your book is still not free, I'd contact KDP via their contact form and let them know that you have made your book free (quote the ASIN) on the other platforms, giving them links to free versions.

With any luck, you should start getting a lot more free downloads, which funnel readers into your paid product(s). Be aware, though, that only a small percentage of freebie downloaders read the book. Therefore, if you can include tempting descriptions to entice them to read the short story, this technique will work better for you.

Book Series?

If you have written a book series (e.g., Zombie vampire killer book 1 – 8), rather than write a short prelude story to the series and give that away for free, give the first book in the series away instead. If downloaders read the first book, they will have invested time in your book and be more likely to order the first and subsequent paid books. However, and this may sound obvious, always make sure there is at least one paid book available for your reader to buy when they finish reading the free one.

Tracking Sales of your Book

You can track sales (and free downloads) of your book by logging into KDP.

Across the top, you'll see a menu:

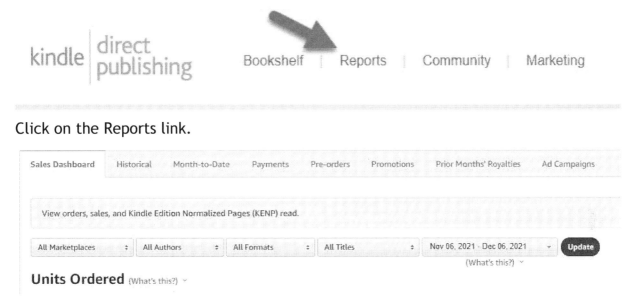

Click on the Reports link.

You have several options across the top of the reports screen.

Sales Dashboard – This screen shows real-time sales of your books. You have a lot of options available to you. For example, you can just look in one of the Amazon marketplaces at a time, or all of them combined. Similarly, you can look at sales of just one book or all books combined. You can also specify the date range.

Data on the sales dashboard is displayed as both graphs and tables. The table at the bottom will give you a quick indication of how much your royalties are going to be, though this table does not include Kindle Edition Normalized Pages (KENP) read. This is the total number of pages read from the borrows of your book. KENP adds a little more to your royalty total.

Historical – This screen shows historical sales and the "KENP read" for your books. Again, you can look at individual books or marketplaces.

Month-to-date – This is a snapshot showing you how you are doing so far this month. It's a table listing your books, units sold, units refunded, KENP read, etc.

Payments – This shows all payments made to you from each of the Amazon marketplaces.

Pre-Orders – Shows details of any pre-orders you may have set up.

Promotions – This screen lists the Kindle Countdown promotions you have made, with a summary table showing how many units you sold at each price increment.

Prior Months' Royalties – This screen shows you the royalties for every month you have been publishing. You can view these online in a table or download the data as an excel spreadsheet.

Ad Campaigns – If you run any Amazon advertising campaigns, you will find details on this tab.

Other eBook Platforms

This book deals with publishing on Amazon only. However, it is worth knowing that there are other platforms where you can publish your eBooks (we mentioned some earlier when discussing Permafree). The thing is, we are using KDP Select on Amazon to offer our books on a 5-day free promo, and while the book is enrolled in KDP Select, you CANNOT publish it in any other digital format. The initial KDP enrollment lasts for 90 days and means you are exclusive to Amazon KDP for those 90 days.

Amazon has it set up so that your books will automatically be re-enrolled once a 90-day period is up, so if you want to cancel KDP enrollment, remember to go in and change the setting manually before the 90-day period is up.

Once you are no longer enrolled in KDP Select, you are free to publish your books on any other platforms you like.

If publishing on other platforms is of interest to you, investigate the following platforms:

1. Apple Books
2. Kobo
3. Barnes & Noble
4. Scribd
5. PublishDrive (Aggregator, distributing books to major retailers)
6. Smashwords (a store in its own right, but also offers global eBook distribution to major retailers and public libraries).
7. Draft2Digital (a distributor of your books).

Non-US Publishers

If you live in the US, then you can ignore this section.

If you live outside the US, then you MUST read this segment.

The number one thing you need to know is that you DO have to declare your Kindle royalties in the country where you live. That means paying taxes where you live on any royalties Amazon sends you. That is **in addition** to what I describe below.

If you live outside the US, then there's another major inconvenience that you have to deal with.

Unless you take action, Amazon will withhold 30% tax on all of your royalty earnings and send them to the US Internal Revenue Service (IRS). It's a double whammy. First, Amazon takes 30% off your royalties and sends you a check for the remainder. You then pay tax in your own country on whatever is left.

OK, so the good news...

If your country of residence has a tax treaty with the US, you can reduce this 30% withholding significantly, even down to zero in some cases (e.g., the UK). To do this, you need to fill out the tax forms on Amazon.

You can submit these online via your KDP dashboard. Click on **Your Account** in the top menu:

On the **My Account** page, scroll down to the bottom, where you should see a section for Tax Information:

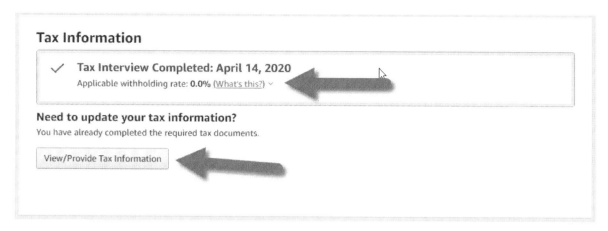

Tax Information

✓   **Tax Interview Completed: April 14, 2020**
Applicable withholding rate: **0.0%** (What's this?) ⌄

Need to update your tax information?
You have already completed the required tax documents.

View/Provide Tax Information

There will be a button to click to **View/Provide Tax Information**.

That will take you through a series of questions you need to answer. At the end of the process, you can submit that information, and Amazon will tell you about your "withholding rate." As you can see in the screenshot above, mine is 0% as I live in the UK.

If you need help with filling the tax forms, you can find sites online that provide some information and help. However, make sure you do this properly, as submitting incorrect information could cause you big problems with the IRS.

Publishing as a Paperback

Hopefully, the first section of the book will have given you everything you need to know about publishing & promoting on Amazon Kindle. Your next step is, if you haven't already done so, is to finish your book and publish it as a Kindle book on Amazon. You'll feel great when you do. But you know what will make you feel even better? Holding a paperback book that you wrote! That is what we are going to do now.

Why a Paperback?

I sell more paperbacks than Kindle editions of my books. That is common for non-fiction writers, less so for fiction writers. However, creating a paperback from your existing Kindle manuscript is easy, so why not? Until recently, Createspace was Amazon's print-on-demand service, but they've now moved it all under the one "KDP" roof. Having both kindle and paperback publishing in the same KDP account makes things even easier. Let's get started.

If you are creating Kindle books, it's relatively easy to convert those books into physical paperback versions without having to pay anything upfront. It works like this:

1. Create your book in the "paperback" format.
2. Submit it for publication.
3. When approved, promote your book.
4. Let Amazon do the rest.

If you make a paperback sale, Amazon prints a copy of your book, then packages and sends it to the customer. At this point, Amazon takes its cut and adds your royalty to your monthly income report.

As you can see, this is pretty much hands-off on your part. All you need to do is promote your book, but Amazon will also do that for you. You don't have to worry about taking orders, shipping, refunds, etc. All you do is collect your royalty payments every month.

This section of the book will take you through the complete process.

You've already created your Kindle book from your Word document, and we'll now use the same Word document to create the paperback version. Most of the work has already been done. All we really need to do is decide on page size, create a cover, and then do some final checks of the document.

How Big Will Your Book Be?

Your book is going to be printed on paper, but what size paper? And what margins do you need around the edges of that paper to make sure text isn't obscured by the spine of the book or cut off during final trimming?

When your book is printed on Amazon, there are costs involved. Printing costs depend on just two things - page count and ink type. Trim size (the book's printed height and width) doesn't directly affect printing costs but does so indirectly because the larger paper will mean fewer pages.

Price Calculator

Head on over to this webpage:

https://ezseonews.com/pricecalc

In the section called **How we calculate printing cost,** there is a link to the **Printing Cost & Royalty Calculator.**

Note: To estimate your printing cost, use our | Printing Cost & Royalty Calculator |

You'll be taken to a web page that offers a calculator.

Calculator

Figures generated by this tool are for estimation purposes only. Your actual royalty will be calculated when you set up your book.

Book Type	Paperback ∨
Interior & paper type	Black & white interior with white paper ∨
Page Count	
Marketplace	Amazon.com ∨
List Price	

Calculate

This is just to give you an idea. The actual costs will be shown when you come to submit your book.

You need three important pieces of information before you can work out royalties:

1. Interior type (Black & White for us).

2. The number of pages.

3. Anticipated list price.

Obviously, the number of pages will be largely determined by your trim size. The larger the trim size, the more content per page, and the fewer pages. You may, therefore, want to play around with the size of the page to see how it affects your royalty.

In Word, on the **Layout** tab, click the **Size** button, and you'll see what size you are currently using:

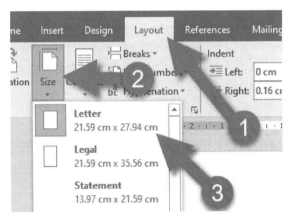

You can also see how many pages Word says the book contains:

This book has 178 pages when it uses a trim size of 21.59 cm x 27.94 cm (my Word is using centimeters, so to convert these into inches, we divide by 2.54). In inches, my trim size is 8.5" x 11.0." Plugging the details into the calculator, my royalty would be around $4.81 per book sold if I charge $12.99:

Marketplace	List Price	Minimum List Price	Printing	Estimated Royalty
Amazon.com	$12.99 USD	$4.98 USD	$2.99 USD	$4.81 USD

If I can reduce the number of pages in the book, I can increase my royalty.

Have a play around with sizes for your books and see how trim size and book-length will affect the royalty you earn. For my book, I am choosing the largest standard format (8.5 x 11) to keep the number of pages to a minimum. You may not be able to do that if you are writing fiction books, as that would just look weird in many cases, but for non-fiction, with 100+ pages, it's fine.

Choose your trim size and set it in Word before continuing.

What About Margins?

Every page in your book will have three outside margins. These margins are important because they ensure the text in your book is not cut off during production.

Amazon gives us guidelines for choosing the correct width of margins based on the number of pages in your book.

Here is the table for the inside margin (where the spine of the book will be):

Page count	Inside (gutter) margins
24 to 150 pages	0.375" (9.6 mm)
151 to 300 pages	0.5" (12.7 mm)
301 to 500 pages	0.625" (15.9 mm)
501 to 700 pages	0.75" (19.1 mm)
701 to 828 pages	0.875" (22.3 mm)

So, for my 178-page book, I need an internal margin of 0.5 inches or 1.27 cm. I'll give it a little more room and set mine to 1.59cm.

The width of your outside margins will depend on whether you have content that "bleeds" to the edge of the page or not. E.g., a picture book where the images go right to the edge of the page without any margin of whitespace.

I am not covering that type in this book, as it is 99% of readers won't need to use that option. Instead, we'll look at the margins for pages with no bleed:

Page count	Outside margins (no bleed)
24 to 150 pages	at least 0.25" (6 mm)(6.4 mm)
151 to 300 pages	at least 0.25" (6 mm)(6.4 mm)
301 to 500 pages	at least 0.25" (6 mm)(6.4 mm)
501 to 700 pages	at least 0.25" (6 mm)(6.4 mm)
701 to 828 pages	at least 0.25" (6 mm)(6.4 mm)

So, my outside margins need to be at least 0.25 inches or 0.64 cm. I'll give it a little more space and set it to 1.0 cm.

Click on **Margins** on the **Layout** tab and choose **Custom Margins** at the bottom of the menu.

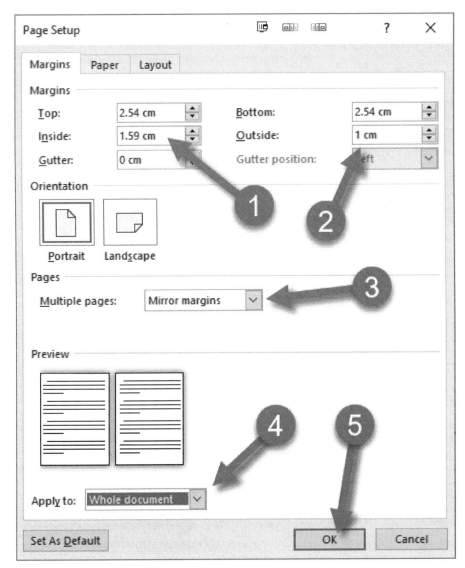

You can find more details on margins (for bleed and no bleed), including videos on changing page size and margins here:

https://ezseonews.com/margin-help

Before continuing, it is important that you have chosen your page size and margins. All the checks we will do need these to be set to the desired values.

Converting to "Paperback" Format

We are going to check the Word document for a few common problems, but before we do, I just want to make sure we are all starting from the same place. You should already have your book written in Word and have it published on Kindle.

After following the previous section of the book, your Word document should have:

1. A title page.

2. Disclaimer / Copyright Information.

3. Table of Contents.

4. Page numbers.

5. All Word styles like Normal, Heading 1, Heading 2, etc. correctly used.

6. A good quality font that you have the license to use in a print book.

Make sure the above checkpoints are all true for your document before you move on.

Before we do anything, save a copy of your Word file as a separate paperback version. That way, any changes you make (and they will be minor) will only affect the paperback version of your book.

Check #1 – Page Size & Margins

Make sure that your Word document is set up to use the correct page size and margins you chose earlier. You can find the settings for these on the **Layout** tab:

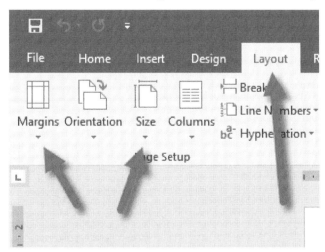

Check #2 – Correct Use of Styles

We need to make sure the styles we have used in our Word document are correct. They should be. After all, you have already published your book on the Kindle platform, and styles needed to be correct there. Nevertheless, go through your document and make sure that paragraphs use the "normal" style, main headings use "heading 1," and so on.

Check # 2 - Links

This check is a simple one too. If you have used hyperlinks in your book, make sure they are short enough for the reader to type into a web browser. Do not create hyperlinks like this because paperbacks aren't clickable. Instead, if it is a short URL that is easy to write, like google.com, then write the full URL. Otherwise, use a link shortener like Google's tool or Bitly.

Check #3 - Numbered Lists

Go through your book and make sure that bullets and numbered lists look OK. Also, make sure that numbered lists start from the right number. If you are making use of the built-in numbered lists in Word, beware. I have had a lot of problems with numbered lists not starting at 1. The list seems to think it is part of a previous list. You'll spot this in your book because your list won't start at number 1.

You can reset the starting number of any list in Word if you find an error.

Also, make sure that if you use bullet lists, they look OK. Sometimes you can find bullet list items that are formatted as child items and indented further than they should be.

Check #4 - Layout

This is a simple check, but an important one. With the Kindle document, the spacing between lines was automatic and simple. The rule was never to use empty lines to space things out. With Kindle, you used the pre-formatted styles like "normal" and "Heading 1" to apply uniform spacing in the document.

The reason for that was the same reason we didn't want page numbers in the Kindle format - Kindles don't have "pages."

Physical books obviously do, so we need to check the layout for a few common problems.

Problem 1 - Empty Lines at the Top of a Page

This should not happen if you have made sure you have no empty lines (remember the pilcrow?), but do go through and make extra sure. I always proof my books with two pages visible in Word and the pilcrow button enabled. Therefore, this type of problem is easy to spot:

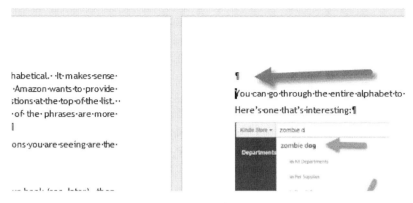

In that screenshot, can you see the gap at the top of the right-hand page?

As you can see, that gap is a misplaced pilcrow and needs to be removed. Go through your document and make sure there are no gaps at the top of the pages.

Problem 2 - Headers at the Bottom of Pages

This problem isn't restricted to headers. It actually includes anything that appears at the bottom of the page but would be better off starting at the top of the next page. For example, here is a header that should be moved to the top of the next page:

That headline is right at the bottom of the page and should be moved onto the next page. There are two ways to do this. Simply add in a line space (yes, a pilcrow), or

same mistakes as these other authors. At the same time, you can include any good ideas.

Have a look to see what other information is available on each of your competitor's product pages. The information changes frequently, but I have covered the main areas that I look at when researching a book. Now, let's find out what the Amazon Best Sellers Rank really means in terms of sales.

Making Sense of the Sales Rank

insert a "new page" break so that the headline appears at the top of the next page. I recommend you use the line space option as it causes less of a problem if you want to use the manuscript to update your Kindle version of the book.

Can you think of other situations that might require an element to be moved onto the next page?

What about this:

So, if you have a sales rank of 10,000, chances are you are selling around 8 - 10 books a day. With a sales rank of around 5,000, that number jumps to 20-25 sales per day. These numbers are only estimates based on my own sales and they are far more conservative than you will get with online BSR calculators you can find online.

I can only guess at sales volume for sellers ranks better than 4,000. After reading other people's experiences, I'd expect something like this:

The page ends with a colon, and the data that the colon refers to is on the next page.

It doesn't look great. This can be OK if the page with the hanging colon is on the left side of the open book, so the reader can see the data on the right-hand page as they are reading the book.

If in doubt, remember that colons like this are usually followed by something important, so it may be best to keep it all on the same page. Add a page break if you can, to make sure the colon is on the same page as the information it refers to.

Check #5 - TOC Update & Check

The next step is to update your table of contents to make sure page numbers are correct. This should always be one of the final checks because if you need to go back in for editing, layout, or page spacing, the page numbers can change for specific headlines and screw up the table of contents. Therefore, complete other checks first, then update the TOC.

Once updated, check to see if you want to edit the TOC further. For example, the pages that appear in your book BEFORE the first numbered page may appear in your TOC and need to be edited out of the TOC. Here is mine for this book:

Contents

Those lines at the top are in the first section of the book before page numbering officially begins. Therefore I'd need to remove those lines from the table of contents, and they can simply be highlighted and deleted. To prevent this from happening, simply do not use Headers in Word for these titles. Use normal text, but make it bigger and bold. It will simulate a headline appearance without being included in your table of contents.

Check #6 - Page Numbers Start on Right-Hand Side

When you publish your book as a paperback, the page numbering MUST start on the right-hand side of the book, like this:

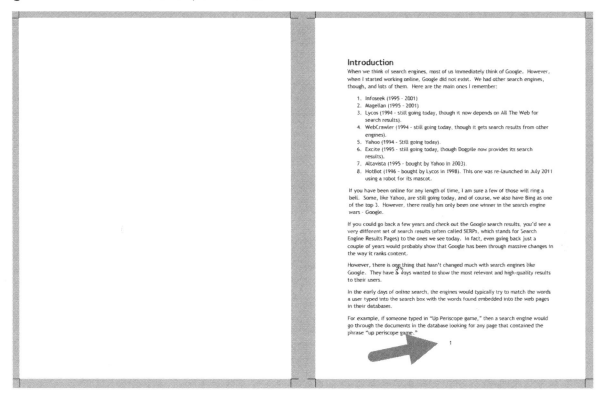

Failure to do so will mean your book will not be accepted by Amazon until you fix it.

Before this first numbered page, you have the title page, disclaimer, table of contents, and maybe some other stuff. It can, therefore, be a little confusing trying to make sure your first numbered page is on the right-hand side. The easiest way of checking this is to count your pages from the beginning. The first numbered page should be an "odd" page (1, 3, 5, 7, 9, and so on).

As I am writing this book, I just checked, and my first numbered page is the 11th page, so I am fine. However, be aware that updating any page before this first numbered page, e.g., TOC, can change the number of pages at the start of the book, so this check should be completed after all others.

Check #7 - Image DPI "Requirements"

When you take a screenshot, the software you use will probably be capturing at between 72 – 100 DPI. DPI is a measure of the number of "dots" that are used in an inch to create the image. When you publish a book on Amazon, they will tell you that you need 300 DPI images, and you do if you want every image crisp. However, that is not possible with screenshots because although you can convert them to 300 DPI, you are converting from 72 DPI, so the image won't be any clearer.

If you have the problem that images are lower than 300 DPI, and you cannot do anything about them, e.g., screenshots, then don't worry about it. You can still publish your book. Amazon calls this a "non-blocking" issue. In other words, the issue won't block the book from publication. The one thing that will help make your images clearer in the final book is to do that black & white conversion we talked about earlier when talking about images.

Images in Word

Word might compress images in your documents, which reduces their DPI. To check and fix this issue, we first need to save the Word document using the Save As button.

In the dialog box that opens, click the Tools menu,

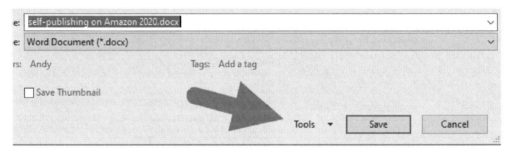

and select Compress Pictures.

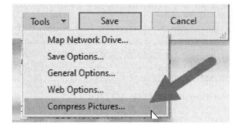

The Compress Pictures dialogue box opens up:

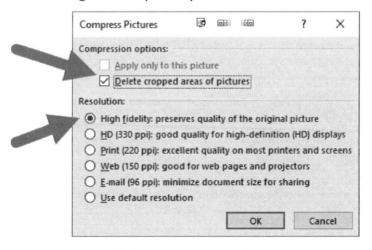

Select the box to delete cropped areas of pictures, and select **High fidelity** to make sure images are not compressed.

Click the OK button.

Now click the **Save** button to save your document.

What we have just done is turn off the compression of images *for this document only*. When you create your next book, remember to save your document this way the first time.

Adding a New Paperback Title

With the book finally ready, it's time to add the book to KDP.

Log in to your KDP dashboard, and you'll see your kindle book already there. Let's upload her big brother. Click on the **Create Paperback** link:

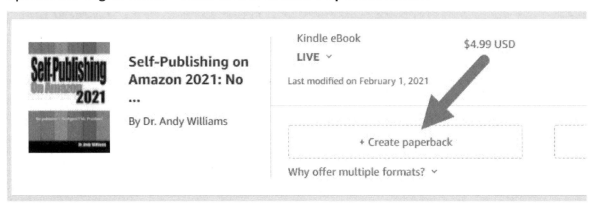

You may be asked to log in again, so do that.

You'll be taken to the **Paperback Details** screen.

This will all look very familiar because you'll have the same fields to fill in as you did for the Kindle.

Since you are adding the paperback version of an existing kindle book, most of the fields will be entered for you.

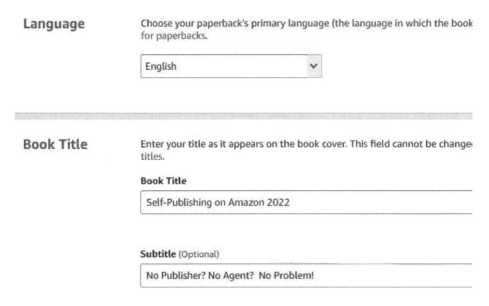

Just go down the page and check everything is in place and correct.

Once the paperback details are complete, click on the **Save and Continue** button.

On the **Paperback Content** tab, the first thing you will need to do is decide on an ISBN number. You can choose to get one for free from KDP or assign one you have bought.

I won't go into the differences here, but for my non-fiction books, I use a free KDP assigned ISBN.

If you want to understand your choices, read this article:

https://ezseonews.com/ISBNChoice

This article refers to Createspace (Amazon's old print on demand service), but the principles are the same.

If you are choosing the free KDP ISBN option, click the **Assign me a free KDP ISBN** button. This will assign an ISBN for your book.

For **Publication Date,** leave it blank. This will be automatically filled in when you click the final "Publish" button.

OK, so now we come onto the **Print Options**. We worked these out earlier in the book. My preferred option is printing on white paper, so my options are as follows:

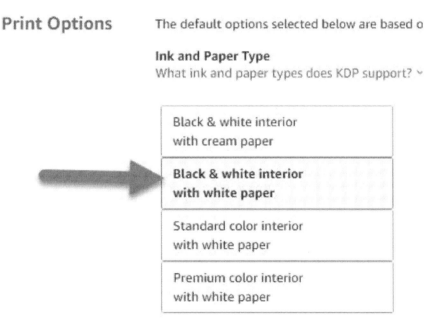

Whether you choose a Matte or Glossy cover is up to you. I have tried both and prefer the glossy look to my books.

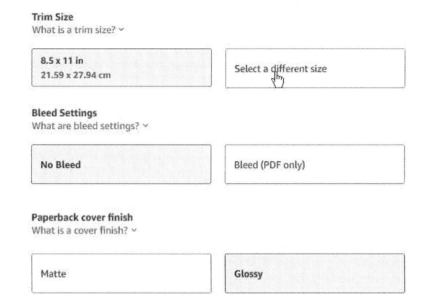

Trim Size
What is a trim size? ⌄

| 8.5 x 11 in 21.59 x 27.94 cm | Select a different size |

Bleed Settings
What are bleed settings? ⌄

| No Bleed | Bleed (PDF only) |

Paperback cover finish
What is a cover finish? ⌄

| Matte | Glossy |

The next section is the **Manuscript**. This is where you upload your book manuscript. I have always preferred the accuracy of uploading a PDF document rather than the Word document. What you see in the PDF document on your computer really is what you will see in the book. When I have tried Word's DOCX formats before, this wasn't the case, and in many cases, the DOCX file failed to be uploaded and converted correctly by KDP. Therefore, I recommend you first save your manuscript as a PDF.

Before we save the manuscript as a PDF, we need to change a setting in Word to embed the fonts in the file.

Click the **File** tab and choose **Options** from the left sidebar:

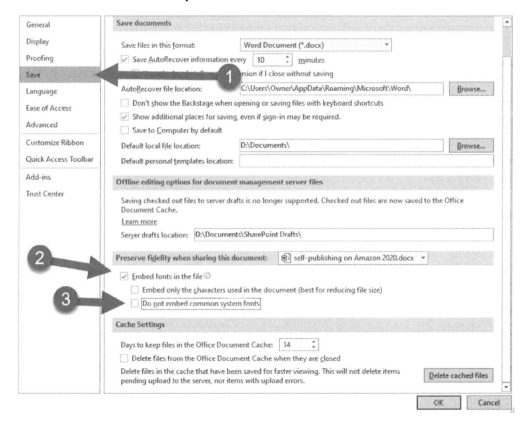

Click on the **Save** tab and check the box to **Embed fonts in the file**. Make sure the two options under this checkbox are both unchecked.

Click **OK**.

You can now save your file as a PDF.

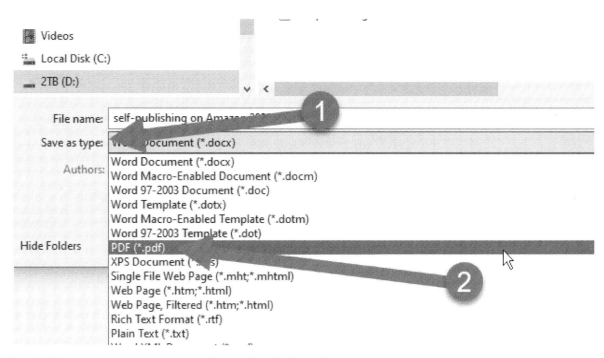

The PDF manuscript can now be uploaded to Amazon.

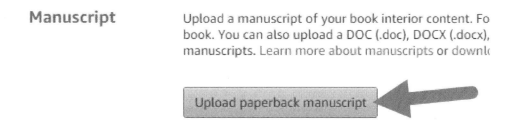

When the file has been uploaded, you will get confirmation. Amazon will then process your file. While it is processing, you can upload your cover.

If you haven't created your cover yet, just scroll to the bottom of the page and click the **Save as Draft** button. You can come back here when you are ready.

Downloading a Cover Template

If you have the skills to design your own cover in Photoshop Elements, Affinity Designer (which I use), or similar, then these instructions will give you the basics. If you believe that you cannot do this yourself, then you might be interested in using Amazon's online cover creator tool.

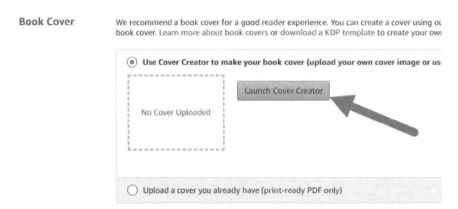

This tool is self-explanatory, so I'll leave you to look at that if you want to.

For the brave authors, I want to give you guidelines on creating your own cover from scratch.

Go to this page:

https://ezseonews.com/KDPCovers

On the left is a form you need to fill in with details of your book print size:

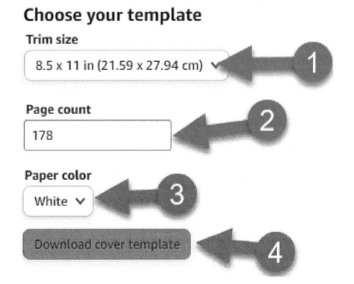

Once filled in, click the **Download cover template** button.

This will download a zip file containing two files. A PDF and a PNG. Both of these are identical in terms of content. You only need to use one. I personally use the PNG graphics file, so that is what I'll cover here.

Extract the PNG file to your computer. The name of the file will give details on the page size and count. My PNG is called **8.5x11_BW_180.png**. That indicates an 8.5 x 11-inch trim with 260 pages in length. The page length will always be a few more than you entered in to the template generator.

The PNG file looks like this:

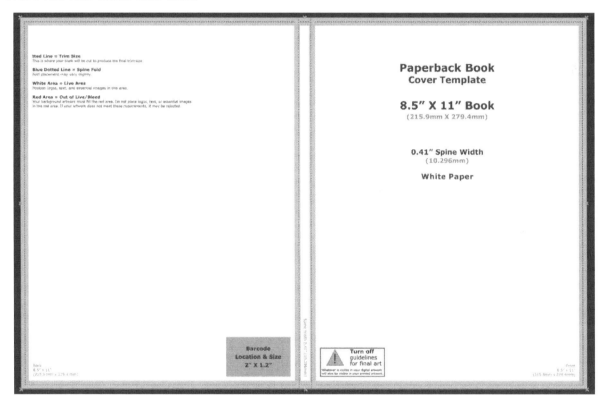

There are clear boundaries for where your cover content should and should not be. Keep content in the white areas.

When adding some content to your cover image, use layers. This will help with editing and making small changes as you work on your cover.

Understanding the Book Cover Templates

You can load the PNG file into any image software, but one that works with layers is recommended. Adobe Photoshop Elements is ideal if you have it. I use Affinity Designer for my covers.

Areas Marked on the Templates

The areas marked on the template are very important because they show you which parts will be used for the front, back, and spine of the cover. If we zoom into the template, we can see this border all around the template perimeter:

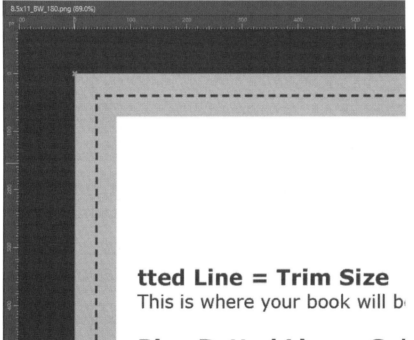

The white parts of the template show you the main content area for your cover. We need to make sure all of the important text, graphics, etc., are contained within the white area.

The black dotted line is where the printers will be *trying* to cut the edges of the cover.

The red areas on either side of this black dotted line are "bleed" areas. These areas MUST not contain anything essential to your final cover design, but they MUST be filled with part of your cover design. When the covers are cut, the cut maybe a little to the left or right of the dotted line. By making sure the bleed area is not empty, the cover will look good even if the cut isn't exact.

Here is an example from one of my own covers:

You can see on the right where the printer should be cutting the cover (the dotted line), but a little to the left, or a little to the right, won't make any difference to the final cover design.

The Spine

Depending on how many pages your book contains, you may be able to fit the title and your author name on the spine of the book. This is what the spine looks like in the template:

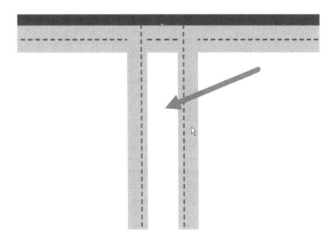

There are two parallel dotted lines running down the middle of the template. These mark the position of folds in the book cover that define the spine of the book. The white area in the middle is the printable area of the spine. Include title and author name inside here if you can. The spine has red bleed areas as well because the fold in the cover may be a little to the right or left. Therefore, text in the spine must not touch the bleed area.

Here is the spine from one of my book covers:

You will notice that the spine text does not touch the bleed area. To the right of the spine, you can see part of the front cover design.

Here is the entire book cover, with elements positioned over the template:

By adding a white background layer over the top of the PNG template, we get to see what the cover will look like on the book:

When the cover is complete, you need to hide the PNG layer before continuing with the processing. That is as simple as unchecking the layer in your editor:

Depending on what tool you are using, the next step is to flatten (& merge) the layers of your image. In Affinity Designer, the first step is to create a Group and drag all the layers inside that group.

You can see that in the above screenshot. I have a group called **Book Cover**, and all other layers (some contained inside groups) are dragged inside the group. I can collapse that Group to be left with just this:

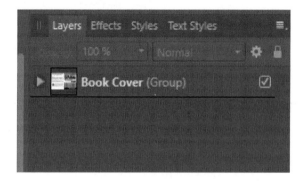

All of the layers making up my image are inside there.

We now need to rasterize this group, which we can do by right-clicking and selecting rasterize:

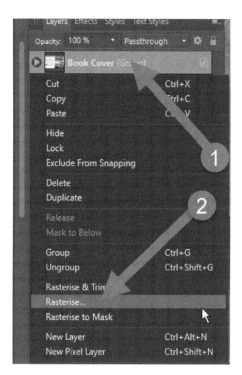

This will create a single layer containing all elements in our design:

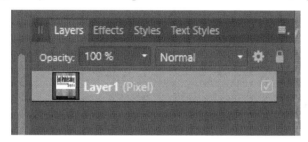

Finally, we can export the cover as a PDF. To do this, select **Export** from the **File** menu.

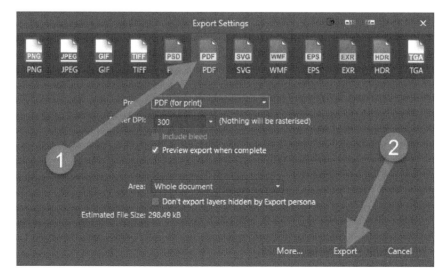

Choose **PDF** as the format, make sure PDF (for print) is selected as the **Preset**, and click on **Export**.

The exported PDF is "print-ready."

Once you have your print-ready PDF cover, click on the **Upload a cover you already have (print-ready PDF only)** radio button, then click the button to **Upload your cover file.**

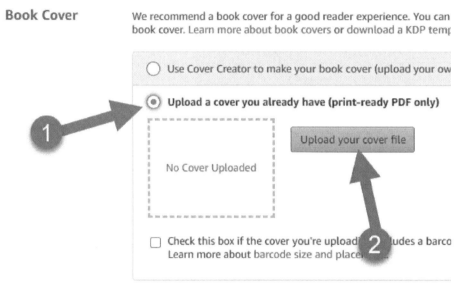

You'll get the message that the cover was uploaded successfully and, of course, that KDP is processing the file. Be patient.

When you are happy that the file has been processed, click on the Book previewer button to see what your book will look like.

A print-ready PDF is created for you to view, but it can take several minutes, so you guessed it. Be patient.

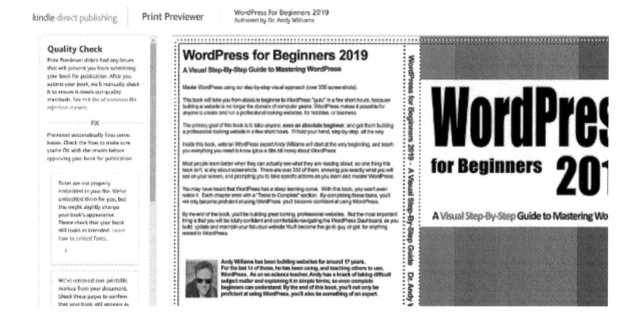

On the left-hand side of the screen is a list of issues you need to work through. The previewer does a good job of fixing most issues, so you may be good to go.

A typical error I get is that fonts were not properly embedded. KDP will do this for you, so it is not something to get overly stressed about. When we saved the PDF, we did tell Word to embed the fonts, so we did all we could there.

Another issue is with non-printable markup:

We've removed non-printable markup from your document. Check these pages to confirm that your book still appears as intended.

1 7 8 9 10 11 12

17 18 21 27 73 79

121 158 189 213

238 239 247

I am not entirely sure about this either, but KDP tells me the page numbers where it removed non-printable markup. Click each page number to make sure your book still looks as it should. If it does, don't stress over this. Everything will be OK.

Go through the entire document in the previewer. Check TOC page numbers against a few of the page numbers in the book to make sure these are all OK. Check everything.

I recommend you download a PDF proof and check it on your computer very carefully. To do that, click the link top right:

Get help
Provide us feedback
Download a PDF proof

Go through the PDF and re-check everything. This is how your book will look when printed.

Once you are happy, you can **Approve** the book by clicking the button at the bottom right of the previewer.

If you decide you need to make more edits, click the exit previewer button to close the previewer and go back to the **Paperback Content** section.

You will need to approve your submission before you continue.

Once you click on the **Approve** button, you'll be taken back to the **Paperback Content** tab. At the bottom of the page, you'll see the actual printing costs for the various marketplaces:

OK, click on the **Save and Continue** button to proceed with your submission. This will take you to the **Paperback Rights & Pricing** screen.

Paperback Rights & Pricing

At the top of the screen, you need to select the territories you want to publish the book in. If you own the copyright of your book, you can publish to all territories:

In the next section, choose your **Primary Marketplace**.

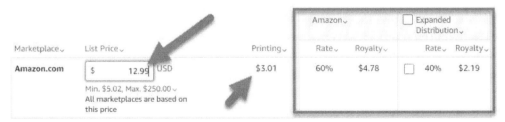

I'd stick with the same recommendation I gave you for the Kindle. If you are not specifically targeting a particular country, leave this set as Amazon.com.

You can now enter your desired price for the book, and KDP will crunch the numbers for you.

Amazon will tell you the printing costs. In my case, $3.01.

You'll see that the royalty rate after printing costs is 60% for books sold on Amazon. So, on my $12.99 book, I'd make $4.78 royalty. That is much higher than traditional printing with a publisher, agent, etc.

You'll notice that there is a checkbox labeled **Expanded Distribution**, with a 40% royalty rate. The 40% royalty relates to books sold through the expanded distribution program, should you choose to use it.

By default, your book will be available on all the Amazon stores where you hold the rights of the book. You choose whether to enroll into Expanded Distribution using that checkbox.

I have mixed feelings about the expanded distribution options. The biggest problem is that an online seller can buy your books at a discount (you get a much lower royalty on these sales) and sell them at lower prices than you do on Amazon, effectively cutting off your sales.

I recommend you do some research on expanded distribution before checking this box. Leave it blank for now. You can come back later once your book is published and change your options here, so don't worry about this.

Personally, I do enroll my books in Expanded Distribution as I feel the added sales to these large book distributors makes sense for me. These distributors can make your titles available to other online retailers, libraries, universities, booksellers, etc.

The table on the Pricing page shows all the other Amazon stores with prefilled values for the price. These prices are calculated from the one you entered into Amazon.com, but you can override the default prices for those stores (if you want to). Personally, I leave these as they are. Amazon works out the equivalent costs in these other currencies, so everyone pays the same for your book, just in their own currency.

Keep scrolling down the page. At the bottom, you have the option to request a proof copy of your book if you wish.

You do have to pay for this, but the costs are much less. For example, with my pricing for the book, people in the UK would have to pay £9.82 (plus shipping). For my proof copy, I pay £2.50 plus shipping:

Request Proof Copies

Order proof copies of your book before publication. Proof copies are printed using your latest uploaded book files which may differ from your book's live version. They will also have a "Not for Resale" watermark on the cover and a unique barcode but no ISBN. You pay only the printing cost for your selected marketplace times the number of copies. Shipping and applicable taxes will be applied at checkout. Learn more

Self-Publishing on Amazon 2022 PROOF:
By Dr. Andy Williams

ORDER QUANTITY

[1 ⌄]   i You can order up to 5 copies at a time

MARKETPLACE OF YOUR ORDER LEARN MORE

[Amazon.co.uk   ⌄]

Total Cost (excluding shipping and taxes): GBP £2.50 (£2.50 x 1)

Does not include shipping and applicable taxes. Within 4 hours of submitting your request, you will receive an email with a link to complete your proof order. Please complete your purchase within 24 hours of receiving this email. Learn more

Be aware that there is no obligation to order a proof copy. I recommend you do the first time you publish a paperback to make it easier to check for errors. However, you can easily check your proofs online using the Amazon Previewer we saw on the Paperback Content screen earlier.

If you decide to order a proof copy, you will then be redirected back to the Pricing & Rights screen.

At this point, you can approve the book if you want to, or wait for your proof copy so you can check it over first. Once you do approve your book, you'll see a screen like this:

Your paperback has been submitted   ✕

Give us your feedback

WordPress for Beginners 2019: A Visual Step-by-Step Guide to Mastering WordPress

By Dr. Andy Williams

$12.99 USD

 Next we'll manually review your book. If it passes our review, it can take up to 72 hours to be available for purchase on Amazon. If it doesn't pass our review, we'll email you. During the review, the book will appear as "In Review" on your Bookshelf. You can change your book details, content, or pricing after the review's done.

Give us your feedback   Done

It is a waiting game now. KDP will email you back once they have manually reviewed your book.

A Proof Copy

If you order a proof copy, expect it in the post within a couple of days. Here is mine:

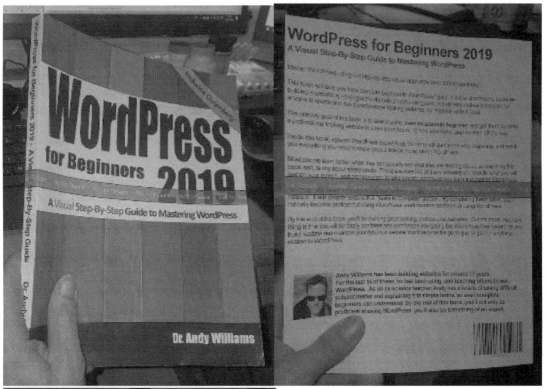

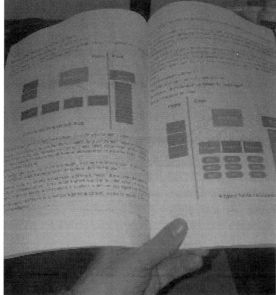

The great thing about these proofs is that you can see exactly how the margins, page sizes, font, images, etc., work together in the final book. If you decide to change anything, you can.

You'll notice that the cover of the proof has a "not for resale" label across the cover (front and back). That reflects the fact you paid a lot less for this copy, with the intention of using it as a proof copy.

Feedback from KDP

OK, your book has either been accepted as is, or you may have some work still to do.

I've had my email back from KDP:

Your Amazon.co... der of "PROOF: Wor...	Amazon.co.uk	19/10/2018, 15:41	
Your paperback book is available in the Am...	Kindle Direct Publishing	20/10/2018, 08:51	

Here are the contents of that email:

Congratulations, the paperback edition of your book "WordPress for Beginners 2019: A Visual Step-by-Step Guide to Mastering WordPress" is live in the Amazon Store. It is available* for readers to purchase here. If you have republished your book, your changes are now live.

*Some marketplaces may take 3-5 business days to show your paperback as in stock. Please note that your paperback's product description may take 24-48 hours to appear on its Amazon detail page and links to its Kindle eBook version may take up to 48 hours. If you are resubmitting your content file or updating your book details, the changes should display within the next 24-48 hours.

Thank you for publishing with Kindle Direct Publishing (KDP).

Best regards,
The Kindle Direct Publishing Team

Great! My book is now in print and available on Amazon, though as it says, it may take 3 - 5 days before your book shows as in stock.

Once it is all ready, you'll find that your kindle and paperback versions appear on the same "sales page" on Amazon, like this:

‹ Back to results

WordPress for Beginners 2021: A \
Mastering WordPress (Webmaster

by Dr. Andy Williams ⌄ (Author) | Format: Kindle Edition

★★★★★ ⌄   13 ratings

Part of: Webmaster Series (8 Books)

› See all formats and editions

Kindle	Paperback
from $5.49	$12.99
Read with Our Free App	2 New from 2.99

Master WordPress using our proven step-by-step visual approach (ov
a major new release for 2021, covering the latest version of WordPres
WordPress during 2021, you can our updates web page for detail
date.

‹ Read more

Print length	Language	Publication date
356 pages ⌄	English	December 20

As you can see, the paperback version is available from the kindle version sales page.

Congratulations, you are now a published author!

Hard Covers?

In 2021, Amazon print-on-demand started offering some authors the option of creating hard covers. I was an early beta tester of this program.

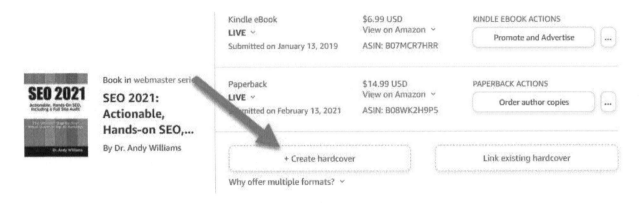

I am not sure if this has been rolled out to everyone yet, so won't be covering this in the book. However, I wanted to offer my thoughts after publishing my WordPress for Beginners book in hardcover format.

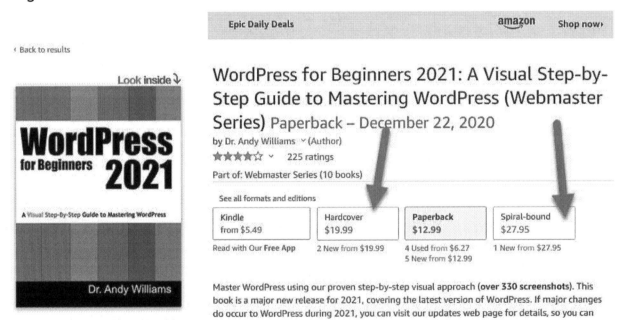

There are a few important points:

1. I make very few hard cover sales compared to paperback. I am sure that if the hard back wasn't available, people would have bought the paperback instead.
2. The extra costs of the hard back means lower commissions. Of course, you can increase the cost of the book to bump up your commission, but that will result in fewer sales. On the hard cover shown in the screenshot, I make $3.45 commission on Amazon.com. Compare that to my paperback, where I make

$3.90 and the cost of the paperback is $7 cheaper.

3. Amazon seems to have created a spiral bound version, which I knew nothing about. I assume this was created with the hard cover version. A spiral bound version could be very useful in some non-fiction genres, but look at the extra cost of that!

4. The only difference between publishing the paperback and the hard back is the cover design. If you want to have a go, search inside your KDP account for **Amazon hard cover template**, and you'll find Amazon's help page on this topic.

Useful Resources

There are a few places that I would recommend you visit for more information.

Grammarly

This is a proofreading/grammar checker plugin for Word. There is a useful free version as well as a fully-featured paid version. Download it and give it a try.

https://ezseonews.com/grammarly

Pro Writing Aid

This is an alternative to Grammarly that I have been using more and more. I like the way you can use the downloadable application to edit documents in other formats, e.g. Scrivener. It also has a Word plugin that offers a lot of features.

https://ezseonews.com/prowritingaid

KDROI

We saw this tool earlier in the book. It helps with setting up promotions for your book. Find out more about this tool here:

https://ezseonews.com/kdroi

Book Updates

When someone buys a paperback, it's impossible for an author to send notifications to the buyer about changes that happen in the publishing process. Therefore, I have set up a page on my website:

https://ezseonews.com/amazon2022/

If anything changes, let me know, and I will update that page with new tutorials so you can keep publishing.

My ezSEONews Website

https://ezSEONews.com – This is my site where I offer free help and advice to webmasters. While you are there, sign up for my free newsletter.

My Other Books

All my books are available as Kindle books and paperbacks. You can view them all here:

https://amazon.com/author/drandrewwilliams

I'll leave you to explore those if you are interested. You'll find books on various aspects of being a webmaster, such as creating high-quality content, SEO, CSS, etc.

My Video Courses

I have a growing number of video courses hosted on Udemy. You can view a complete list of these at my site:

https://ezseonews.com/udemy

There are courses on the same kinds of topics that my books cover, so SEO, Content Creation, WordPress, Website Analytics, etc.

Please Leave a Review/Thought on Amazon

If you enjoyed this book, or even if you didn't, I'd love to hear your comments about it. You can leave your thoughts on the Amazon website.

Made in the USA
Middletown, DE
22 March 2023

27354776R00093